I Quit!

Working For You Isn't Working For Me
Planning Your Great Escape!

Elizabeth Lions

This book is dedicated to Jim Horner, my father, who had the highest work ethic of any individual that I have known.

Table of Contents

Introduction: This book is dedicated to the job seekers who hate where they work and are unsure of how to get out of their current situation. I understand your fear of the future, your concern with stability and your resistance to change. I also have hope that you will choose differently and embrace the life that you would ultimately create. Most of all, I hope I can be the catalyst to your transformation.

This book is for those who just cannot take it anymore. Many of you are what I call the survivors of recession. The looming fear of the unemployment line was never far from your mind. You witnessed firsthand the recession that impacted your family and friends. Someone close to you was laid off and you watched them tick away weeks of unemployment while staring at online job postings, hoping for a call to interview. Quietly, slowly, steadily, you kept your job and went to work each morning.

You survived the ten to fifteen percent pay cuts that were never reinstated by your company. You took the reduction in pay gladly because you thought you wanted to keep your job. Most of all you just did not want it to happen to you.

Each day you went to work, despite the headlines in the papers reporting more layoffs and budget cuts. You read about all of the new grads unable to find work. You marched through fear. You held the company together when you did not think you could. There were days the pressure was insurmountable. Determined, you went quietly to your office each morning, hoping not to highlight your attendance in any negative way that would cost you your job. You worked longer hours and saw your family less. Most of all, you were thankful because you got to keep your job and make your house payments, telling yourself you were the lucky one.

You scaled back where you could, stopped going on expensive vacations and quit eating out. The months ticked by and still you continued working, tirelessly, hoping the market would turn around. You hoped your 401(k) would go back up. Headlines claimed that recession was over, but the truth was there was nobody left to layoff.

You ended up doing three people's jobs—Bob's, Mary's and Steve's. They were all laid off and you watched as the cubes around you emptied. Yet you remained standing. There was no other job 'out there' to rescue you from the struggling organization you were single-handedly holding together. It was like a game of musical chairs and everyone sat down when the music stopped. But the seat you sat in was hard, cold and uncomfortable.

Now that the dust has settled, you wonder if this is all there is to life.

What qualifies me to stand before your presence in this manner is my background. For more than a decade, I was a prominent headhunter on the west coast, that worked with the glitzy high tech and manufacturing companies. I sat with your boss, through meeting after meeting, and discussed your performance while he evaluated if you would make the cut.

I had the honor and privilege to be a part of building teams in organizations, by helping a leader evaluate and ultimately staff top talent. I have witnessed not one, but two recessions.

After being unemployed for eighteen months, grown men have sat with me at the local Starbucks and cried, wondering if they would ever get their lives back. I have helped the woman who knew she would get divorced, but needed a better income in order to exit her marriage, to transition. I've worked with people who sat in jobs they hated, stewing over the petty comment made in the morning's staff meeting. I worked with clients that suffered heart attacks because of work related stress, and then came to me for council.

I have worked with people from the very top, to mid-level managers in large organizations, and even with small privately held organizations. *I am the keeper of their secrets.* A trusted soul, whose intention is to give back by sharing those experiences with a willing audience that is seeking a change. It's time to get off the merry-go-round of chaos.

Through all of this listening, I have deep compassion for others, and for that I am eternally grateful. I realized we are never alone; we are constantly connected. Through my own career path, I have witnessed the human spirit. I know what a person can go through, and what they can become. I have an unusual vantage point, and I am so thankful for my own career due to the satisfaction I derive from it.

In 2009, while I was recovering from cancer, I wrote my first book, "Recession Proof Yourself" which was designed to help people who lost their jobs in the great recession. This book is for those that hate being where they're at, and need to find something better—quickly.

Staying in a job that you hate zaps your energy. All energy is creative, and when channeled, it can grow to an amazing level. The energy that you have is your birthright, and when aligned with the right company, phenomenal things can happen. The energy exchange is twofold; you devote your time and talent, and the company pays you and is profitable. At least, that is how it is supposed to work.

Once you make the decision to leave, change starts to happen everywhere in your life. For one thing, you no longer come home tired after a full day of work. You have energy to give back to your family and your hobbies. You feel valued. Co-workers don't get to you as much. Life is more vibrant and fluid. On the contrary, being at a job you hate makes you recoil from life. Your energy pulls back and you have to conserve and preserve...yourself. Clients have described the feeling of being in the wrong job as having their soul sold for a paycheck. It's painful, and I am here to tell you that such suffering is optional, not required.

No stock has ever raised two points due to its employees being in constant fear or loathing.

Energy is collective. Align yours to a place that benefits both you and the employer. Conduct your job searches differently, with your talents and values in mind.

What have you learned though this traumatic experience called recession?

Are you ready to tell the truth about who you really are?

Are you ready to choose?

This book is different than other career books on the shelf in that it was written by someone who has been there, experienced what you have and gets it.

As the reader, you also stand to capitalize on my previous experience as a headhunter, which spanned more than a decade. The bottom line is I know why the company kept you, and fired "Bob". I know whether or not you will get promoted. I know the next steps in your career path, and I know all of this because I was the woman in town who got the call from your boss. He told me all the dirty little secrets in the organization that caused you to be hired, or fired or promoted. I have witnessed all political games played. I was paid to find better chess pieces for the game of business.

There are days I wish I did not know so much. As the keeper of the secrets, I know which company's stock is about to fall before the morning paper can report it—by the attrition that occurs or the new CFO that takes the reins.

Today you have your own secret; your big secret job search.

Job searches should be confidential, meaning only those that truly support your highest vision are included. Be cautious, and evaluate who surrounds you. I don't recommend telling co-workers that you are looking for another job. Things could erupt and go the wrong way if you share your exit plan.

Who are those that support your highest vision? Your family may be on the list, along with friends outside of work. Notice who is in your life right now that you deem closest to you. Are these people supportive of your highest vision, or threatened by it? If they support your highest vision, then share the job search with them. They will carry the vision with you collectively until you step into it on earth plane.

If people around you aren't supportive, protect your vision of leaving for greener pastures. Keep creating inside what it would feel like to find a place that made you feel valued. There is nothing better than working hard and feeling that you contributed at the end of the day.

As a confidential candidate, when you read this book you will learn how to align yourself with the right employer, through examining your core values. You'll slow down long enough to examine what is really important to you, and choose the next job wisely, instead of running out of corporate America only to go stumbling into yet another dissatisfying job. As the reader, you'll learn how to conduct your post-recession job search, how to negotiate your wages without breaking into a sweat, and how to leave your current position with grace.

You are not alone.

In May of 2011, Forbes conducted a survey, finding that Boomers (ages 48-65) were the unhappiest at work, followed by Gen X (ages 32-47). Of Boomers, 65% are planning to leave their current jobs, while 28% of Gen X will be looking for another opportunity.

In January of 2011, CNN surveyed 1400 workers in the United States and found that 84% are fed up and looking.

According to a recent survey by the job placement firm Manpower, 84% of employees are updating their resumes and looking for another career path.

Why is America so unhappy at work? The surveys found that workers feel stagnant, unable to move ahead, and were disappointed with their leadership overall. Half of those surveyed reported that promotion was the most effective way to retain them in their current positions. Equally, 43% stated that support and appreciation from the higher ups was as important to them as increased compensation. The American workforce is disillusioned and frustrated, tired of working long hours without a thank you or an additional day off through the recession.

Time is on your side. Thanks to all of your patience and waiting...the tides are about to turn.

Any economist will tell you that recession runs about a 10-12 year cycle as it moves from a bear market to a bull market. A bear market is defined as a prolonged period in which investment prices fall, accompanied by widespread pessimism. If the period of falling stock prices is short and immediately follows a period of rising stock prices, it is instead called a correction. Bear markets occur when the economy is in recession or unemployment is high, or when inflation is rising quickly. The most famous bear market was in the 1930's, followed by the great recession in 2009.

During a bear market there are few jobs and many candidates. Competition is high and unemployment is high. Managers have many different candidates to choose from in the hiring process, which causes confusion and indecision.

A bull market is defined as a prolonged period in which prices rise faster than average as a result of an economic recovery, economic boom or investor psychology. The longest and most famous bull market occurred in the early 1990's in which U.S. equity markets grew at the fastest pace ever.

During a bull market there are many jobs and few candidates. With talent driving the market, the employers find if they don't extend offers quickly, they lose the candidate to another offer. These 'hot' candidates end up with multiple top dollar offers by numerous employers, giving them the power of choice. America has seen this trend previously. For example, in Silicon Valley during the dot-com boom, employers were fighting for talent and losing the war.

Tick tock. Those who survived recession don't have to take it anymore. As the job ads multiply, fewer candidates apply and there you are!

The time is now; you need to learn and position yourself to maximize the flood of jobs about to erupt in the market in the next couple of years.

As you will notice, this book is written in three parts, each from a different perspective, so you can see the whole picture and ultimately the game that is being played. The three parts of the book are: You (the candidate), Them (the employer) and Us (the headhunter).

Part One (the candidate) is meant to be the longer section. All change starts with you. We cannot change the employer's hiring process or their thinking, nor can we change how a headhunter operates in their business, but we can control the way you relate to the job hunt. It all starts with you owning the responsibility of the job search and making your choices.

This book is unique in that I illustrate what each party in the hiring process thinks, in hopes that this will afford you a new mindset in the job search. You will no longer wonder what the prospective boss could be thinking in an interview. Questions about how headhunters are motivated will be answered. Finally, the mystery of how to conduct a proper job search is over, for all the answers are here. The market and the job search have changed in the last ten years, and you have to understand the game in order to play. Those who think (and operate) as if it is 1999 will be left behind.

I was compelled to write this book to arm you with information that could change your life. Very little information about what I discuss is out there in a public forum. Oddly enough, people who write about me often refer to me as the 'recovering headhunter'. I guess that is accurate. Along with practical how to tips, I also share stories of people just like you who long for another job, but aren't sure how to go about getting one. My intent is for you not to feel alone.

If you are not looking to change your life, do not read this book. This is for people who are tired of having the same experience at work over and over again and that are willing to do something different. Minimally, they think it could be *possible* to have a better life, which includes changing their career.

It doesn't matter if you are 30 or 50; this advice is universal and works no matter where you're at in your career. This is about transformation and owning your power. Playing the victim to your job, being a slave to your health insurance and 401 (k) is no longer necessary. There is another job out there for you, and it's in a place where you can feel worthy and give all of what you have to offer.

This book is about breaking the cycle. Awareness begins with you.

Are you ready and willing?

Chapter 1
The Grand Illusion

We <u>all</u> lie.

We lie about who we are, keeping ourselves in a prison of fear.

We fear that if we tell the truth about who we were, no one will like us. We lie to ourselves. We lie to the world, marketing ourselves as a different person, projecting what we think we should be, rather than being authentic. We live in isolation. We are our own secret.

We especially lie in interviews. We tell the employer exactly what we think they want to hear in order to choose us. It becomes all about being picked, instead of being honest, true, authentic and revealing. It takes a lot of guts to be honest with our values, skills, strengths and inherent weaknesses. Most of us will not risk it. We just want another job, hoping it will get better. Surprised, we move from position to position, each time thinking it will be a different experience. But there is no such thing. The results never quite pan out. If we exercised diligence in the initial interview process, we would have a different result.

I have witnessed this scenario play out too many times, and I know this to be true. I have worked with thousands of individuals in transition, each with a vastly different skill set. From C level executives to entry-level managers, I have held thousands of conversations with people who were unhappy at work and yet they kept repeating the pattern U.U. equity markets grew. After my first book, *Recession Proof Yourself* went national; I started getting calls from all over the country. It was clear to me that I hit the nail on the head with my observation; people are unhappy at work. Whether it's a bull market or a bear market, everyone is searching for something more, but they are not sure what it is. Unable to define 'it' they drift. Drifting causes the spirit unease.

The purpose of this book is to illustrate a new way to approach a job change. It's a guide that encourages you to know who you are *first*, and then decide who you want to be <u>*in relation*</u> to your career. Although that sounds simple, we rarely conduct our job searches like that. We go from job to job thinking, "Surely this company *will be different...*" only to find that wherever you go, there you are.

This book reminds you that <u>you</u> are the constant. It reinforces that you are the constant that moves from place to place, job to job and boss to boss. Most of all, this book will encourage you to be who you are and not to change that piece. Being anchored in who you are will produce a different outcome in the job search.

I am the lucky one, although it took me years to get here and to say that. I do what I love for a living. I am an author, an Executive Coach and a trusted consultant to large corporations. It is through listening to others and finding my own path that I have gained the credibility to teach what I have learned. I have designed a unique program that works for people in transition whether they are unemployed or employed. All of my clients come to me on referral, and they are all unhappy at work. Together, we figure out why. When working with a client who wants to make a job change but seems uncertain, we spend the first few sessions discovering who they are, who they are not, and who they want to be. It is personal and private. I always find myself in quiet amazement of them, and I feel honored to witness their process.

It takes a lot of bravery to be candid with me, basically a stranger, but my willingness to listen with my mind and heart reaches them intuitively; they know how much I care.

To tell the truth, I am obsessively curious about people and why they do what they do. I want to know who they are so that I know what I'm working with. I'm not judging, rather, I'm assessing. Monitoring how far I can push them and determining whether or not they really want to walk down this path with me. I listen to them with the perspective of an employer and try to uncover what parties of them are really marketable. I'm thinking ahead about how we can package that in the interview.

I warn each client that they will not be the same after the program is completed. My favorite part of this work is witnessing the imperfections in people as well as their shine. Imperfections do not deter me. I welcome them, for I want to see the *real* them.

I need to see beyond the lie.

I need to see beyond the projection of *who they would like me to see.*

I need truth. It is the only way I can help them. I must work with the authentic person and not the market version of them.

Looking back on my own life, the option of telling the truth was instilled in me as a child. I will never forget the day I stood before my mother and lied. I cannot remember what it was over, exactly. Frightened of being caught, I looked her dead in the eye and lied.

In retrospect, I feared her rage, which is what ultimately made me lie. Hell hath no wrath like my mother's. Her anger scared me to my core. This is a woman who could raise one eyebrow and make me nearly wet myself. This was back in the olden days of parental boundaries and respect. Mom didn't need to be liked; she insisted she was respected. She told me once that she had plenty of friends, so that tactic was out. Nope, Mom was known to flare up at any moment with her Irish temper. Highly intuitive at a young age, I could judge what the night would be like in my house when I hit the front door coming home from school. And this particular day would be no different as I felt the grip of sheer panic overcome my little body. Sternly she looked at me and said, "Elizabeth, you won't get into trouble if you tell the truth. I will not punish you. But I will not tolerate a lie. If you tell the truth, you'll always be protected. Now, I'm going to ask you again, did you do that?"

Quickly I calculated my options. If I lied and she figured it out, I would be in big trouble. If I told her the truth, it was conceivable that I would get off the hook. One option was a surefire path to punishment, the other a gamble. I swallowed hard and trusted her. I told the truth.

To my utter amazement, she did not punish me, and that day colored my entire adult life. I am certain that if my mother were alive, we would have a good laugh, and I often wonder if she would remember it the way I do. I am sure she had no idea the impact she had on me. That conversation changed my perspective forever. As an adult, I still follow the belief that if I tell the truth I am protected, and that if I follow the rules I will always be okay. She taught me to color within the lines of justice and to see the value in knowing my rights.

She taught me about accountability, and that it was much easier to take responsibility than lie and weave a fabric of guilt that would follow me. Suffice it to say, I sleep well at night and I have been known to dump my guts to the cop that pulls me over for a speeding ticket.

I value, above all, truth and trust. It is my firm belief that truth and trust are the core components of any relationship. Yet it is a small wonder that we do not tell the truth.

Have you ever heard the expression 'hedge your bets'? It originates from an accounting term called hedging, and is used when trying to calculate a commodity with pricing that goes up and down. Accountants will 'hedge' and use that number for projections. It is an art and an educated guess. It is also what I do in my own practice. I hedge people instead of numbers. I take an educated guess about who they really are before they tell me. I determine their strengths and their flaws as I listen. I look for the flinch point and dare myself to get close to it, knowing that is the pinnacle of real growth. I sit in wonder, hoping they will be brave enough to reveal themselves to me so that I can help them find the right job. I know that honesty builds in small increments. Trust builds when you tell the truth and realize that nothing bad happens to you. We all fear that we'll be viewed as terrible, and to our surprise when we find out that the person on the other end doesn't judge us, we gain courage. Perhaps, it may even allow us to forgive ourselves for past mistakes.

Awareness is the first key to change, and typically that is when I get the call. It's that Wednesday afternoon when your boss kicked you for the last time. You think through what went wrong in the current job and why you are so unhappy. And I mean the *real* reasons. Perhaps it is the relationship with the boss that is not working and finally you are strong enough to end a toxic relationship.

Or, perhaps the job is no longer challenging and boredom has set in. For some, the company culture does not resonate with them any longer, like a marriage that after ten years feels mismatched. The employee grew, but the company did not grow at the same rate the employee did. Over time, the energy builds and dissatisfaction engulfs you. Each day the alarm goes off and you dread the day ahead.

Know the difference between the illusion and the truth. Make no mistake; the illusion holds you apart from the truth. It's the movie in your head that paints a picture separate from the reality of your life. The illusion can be sound and logical, like the looming voice in your head. It is the subtle lie you tell yourself. It is so sneaky and so quiet you don't even know it is there.

It has a voice inside your head and it sounds like this:

This job is fine for now. It is not the time to look for another one. The market is tight. With so many candidates why would they want me? I can hang on a little longer. Maybe I will get my ten percent back this quarter.

Really? Did they give it to you back last quarter? What are you waiting for?

What is the *real reason* you are afraid to move forward?

If you are considering a job change, you are not alone. Employees—including executives—are just itching to leave their jobs. Workers today feel dissatisfied, regardless of their level.

Right Management, a well known outplacement firm, stated in November of 2009 that sixty percent of employees intend to leave their jobs as the economy improves, and an additional twenty-seven percent are networking or have updated their résumés, according to a survey of nine-hundred and four workers in North America.

What's more a study of 1,627 employed executives from consulting firm Finnegan Mackenzie, and business network ExecuNet, found that more than ninety percent of executives would take a recruiter's call, and more than fifty percent are looking for a new job. That is a strong statement. And that was in 2009, in the heat of recession.

The statistics today certainly paint a picture that workers are unhappy and that things have taken a turn for the worse.

In July of 2011, CareerBuilder conducted a study that stated seventy-seven percent of workers say they are burned out in their jobs, and forty three percent of workers say their stress levels on the job have increased over the last six months.

Employees are clearly expressing their pent-up frustration with how they have been treated through the downturn. While employers may have taken the necessary steps to streamline operations to prevent going bankrupt, employees may have felt neglected in the process. The result is a disengaged and disgruntled workforce.

Employers are asleep at the switch. The ExecuNet/Finnegan Mackenzie study found that professionals at all levels of management are misjudging the percentage of direct reports interested in pursuing new opportunities. Accountability for executive retention also appears to be missing, with only six percent of CEOs reporting that losing a top executive would hurt their pay or bonus, the study discovered.

I encourage you to just take a look and see what is out there. The illusion is an insidious way of keeping you 'safe'. The reality of the illusion is that you never really are safe. Safe is a relative term, and frankly, your employer is not responsible for that.

You are responsible for your career path.

I will illustrate this point a bit further.

No one is responsible for your happiness but you.

It is not up to your wife/husband/sister/brother/mother/father/aunts/uncles/kids/co-workers/neighbors or boss to make you happy.

Therefore, if your job no longer makes you happy, it is up to you to get out of it.

The illusion tells you that it's the bosses' fault that you are not successful. The illusion allows you to dodge the responsibility of owning your career path. It's the easy way out. Pass the blame around rather than get online and look for a new job. The illusion tells you it is not a good time to find another job and you can hold on. The illusion tells you to be loyal and responsible to your family, bring home a steady paycheck and put your own needs aside. The illusion tells you that you are too tired to come home from work and look for another job.

The illusion also tells you that if you did have the nerve to go out and find another job you would have to sell your skill set. You cannot really be you. You cannot really be forthright and tell the potential employer who you are and what you are willing to do. You cannot tell them that your current boss is certifiably crazy or that you lost commitment to the company months ago. During the throes of recession, you were the last man/woman standing, but now you are weary. You doubt who you are, what skills you have and where you can take them next. Most of all, you loathe the routine of applying online.

The voice of doubt creeps in and asks, "How will you know if it is the right job?"

How will you know that you are not signing up for the same sort of company, or that this new job won't be equally awful? At least this is the devil you know.

Change is a funny thing. It seems the longer a person resists making a change, the harder it is to implement when change becomes necessary. Over the years I worked with clients who were grossly, obviously, painfully unhappy at work and resisted finding another job. The excuses were because they hadn't done a job search in five years, or in a decade, or whatever the timeline. You get the point. Clients will actually say to me, "Well, I'm a little afraid. I haven't looked for a job or been interviewed in years. I have no idea how to do that."

Is the incessant drive to keep things stable overriding your ability to seek change, just because you have not made a change in a long time?

We fear the interview the most because we actually have to talk about ourselves. We know we are unhappy, but do not want to talk about <u>why</u> we are unhappy at our job.

No employer wants to hear the ugly truth, right? And especially not in an interview.

The illusion tells you that you have to sell skill, but your intuition cannot deny that if you keep conducting the job search like you did, you will always get what you have gotten. *You already know this on some level.* You know that if you go into another interview and discuss your skills, as opposed to who you are, it will be the same experience, just in a different building. A good friend of mine used to say, 'Same circus, Elizabeth, just different clowns.'

I am boldly stating that you can be yourself. Individualism is the only way to go because the tribe will no longer protect you. You are no longer their responsibility.

You can tell the truth about who you are and discuss the skills that you have acquired over the years. This time you can choose to conduct the job search differently.

If you continue to do what you have done, you will always have the same experience.

Telling the truth about who you are will produce a different result.

Conducting the job search with your values and career goals in mind will bring a refreshing change. In fact, you will finally find an organization where you enjoy working, instead of just funding your 401 (k) and taking home a paycheck. You will have to be willing to conduct the entire job search process differently, with a combination of data gathering and ensuring your emotional needs are met.

Notice I stated that your emotional needs should be met, but that is not the primary focus.

If you focus on the emotional needs completely, you will make career choices that are not financially profitable or smart for your retirement. If you make career decisions based solely on your salary and benefits, you will find your wallet fat, but your emotional health diminished. This is why people hit the snooze button at six AM as they dread getting out of bed for another day of work. Their emotional values are not met. Or, they have a heart attack at fifty. On the opposite end of the spectrum, if you are doing a 'feel good' job in non-profit, it makes sense to think about the health of your bank account for the future. There is no bitter pill quite like that of regret.

You could choose to do this job search differently and stop suffering. Look at your resume. Think about the last ten years. What did you accomplish that you are proud of? What did you do that you wish you had done differently?

I am no different from you. I do this work for many reasons, and after ten grueling years as a headhunter, seeing not one but two recessions, I realized that like everyone else, I did not like what I did for a living. Every time I made a placement I would hum the bluesy tune, "The Thrill Is Gone", and no matter what I did, I could not get the feeling back. While years ago I craved the hunt, I was no longer hungry. I guess I grew out of it. It was disturbing. Here I was with a great reputation and I did not want to do this anymore. After a lot of careful introspection and consideration I realized I do not enjoy finding jobs for other people, but what I do love is to witness a person's transition.

I enjoy teaching, training and working in corporations with management teams. But most of all, I like to see individuals in that pivotal point of change, when their lives are in ashes and uncertainty looms around them. I love seeing them begin in darkness and then watch them as they re-create their lives. I have been fortunate enough to partner with people, ask questions and hang around long enough to see what they choose. It is a gift to be trusted and have people disclose their biggest fears to you in a coffee shop, hoping no one around them can hear the conversation.

The ability to quickly assess a situation and predict how one 'ticks' comes eerily easy to me. The gift is a curse that also allows me to make quick, absolute judgments about people and about what comes next. I am an endless "What If" scenario running in the background of a large mainframe called life. I am almost always right in my assessments of people.

I said *almost* always right. Sometimes I am wrong. What I have learned is I know nothing.

In conducting this work, I am forced to stay in the realm of what is possible, for at any moment any one person can choose and choose again, making my calculated judgment about what could happen...incorrect. I get to live in a "What If" world with no prescribed conclusions, walking side by side with someone in free will. Yes, I get to witness them stepping away from the tribe, out of safety and into their calling. While I can guide and give fact driven market data on what happens, still there is a margin of error called human possibility.

In the job search, scars are revealed, hurts are healed and explored, and then, in time, when they are ready we make some decisions about what to do next. This is not my place to advise, but to listen, as a partner who gently pushes them forward, always wondering with heart pounding excitement what will they choose? What will they do next? Who will interview them? Where will they land? Knowing all the time that this next job will be better for them if they just show up and do the work.

So in case you are wondering, that is the pleasure I get out of my job.

That is my truth, why I write and why I am here.

Think about who you really are, what you are really good at and what you hate doing. I am not suggesting that you pitch your entire career, but examine who you are in relation to work.

You can lie to one. You can lie to another.

But don't lie to yourself.

Being dishonest with yourself will leave you emotionally bankrupt.

Chapter 2
The Combination of Truth, Talent and Values

One morning over coffee, my husband asked a brilliant question: "Why is it that we go to work and expect to be happy? Why is that? Did you know that thirty years ago you worked for eight hours, got your pay on Friday and had your weekends off? There wasn't some happy crappy consultant like you that came in and taught large companies how to retain their employees. We *were* happy years ago. We took our pay, went to the bar or a bowling alley on Friday nights, bought a little boat or a new car, took vacations and that was it. *When did all of this change?*"

I was a bit startled by what he said because it did beg an answer. I can only begin to guess that it started for us in the Nineties when the dot-com boom started to infiltrate the West Coast. People worked long hours in this magical arena called "high tech", where you could make a million dollars over night out of virtually nothing. It was a new, virtual world, and a person could have a business made out of nothing but a website. CEO's were not grey haired guys, but instead energetic thirty-somethings. Venture Capitalist money flowed like red wine in Napa Valley. On any given Tuesday morning, with little warning, the receptionist who made a forty thousand dollar salary could suddenly become an overnight millionaire as the stock went public. Americans bought stocks, watched them climb and thought it would last forever. If you were not in, you were out, and no one wanted to be out. It was a time of great possibility, hope and prosperity, all built from a fictitious storefront held on the Internet. Experts worried brick and mortar stores would become dinosaurs and no one would shop in malls anymore.

Companies wooed candidates with stock options, large cafeterias with endless supplies of soft drinks in the fridge and foosball tables in the conference rooms. Companies started to look more like college campuses, with all the conveniences of home. After a long day at work, returning to your apartment in Silicon Valley paled in comparison.

As the old adage states, what goes up must come down, and that is exactly what happened. The bust of the dot-com proceeded, making us all reevaluate what was really important to us. We wondered if this was all there was in life, and if work was the be all and end all. Yet, we had to support ourselves somehow and could not figure out how to get off the merry-go-round. Not working wasn't an option. Partially because we had bills to pay, but we also developed a hankering for the lifestyles we created and to the money we had earned. We started to wonder how much was, frankly, too much, and if it was all worth it?

We spent the last fifteen to twenty years building skill sets, chasing the designations, the certificates, and the classes only to wake up and find ourselves fantastic on paper, but unhappy in reality. We learned how to sell our wares, if you will, at the interview. Books were written about behavioral interviews and taught candidates how to navigate if the line of questioning went beyond your skill level and danced upon your personal habits.

There is a big correlation between being happy at work and telling the truth about who you are.

Look at the data.

A survey conducted in 2010 for the Conference Board, a management research organization, found that the drivers of the drop in job fulfillment included less satisfaction with wages and less interest in work. In 2009, 34.6% of workers were satisfied with their wages, down more than seven percentage points from 1987. About 51% in 2009 said they were interested in work, down nineteen percentage points from 1987. This is data that proves my husband Steve's theory. Life was simpler and we were happier at work. Why did it all change? How did it change? Did WE change?

But the biggie; will we ever be happy at work again?

Data points out that few of us are happy and that we are constantly seeking a work/life balance, but we never seem to reach our destination. However, after over a decade of working with individuals in job transition, I have arrived at a theory and a solution. Here is my bold concept:

Let's all stop flinging our skill sets.

Seriously! Let's stop talking endlessly about our skills and slow down long enough to think about who we are *in addition to* our skills.

You don't think you're a robot, clicking out bits of information in a cube, do you? Who are you as a person? What do you *value* in work? What makes you feel like a part of the team? What makes you excited about the company's success? What makes you feel as if you've contributed something larger than your skill? When was the last time you put your heart, mind and soul into a project and felt great about the work you did?

Through the years I have concluded that there is a dramatic disconnect during the interview process. We get caught up in talking about our C++ / Excel / ACT /Word/Accounting/People Management skills (or whatever skills you are parading out there) that we don't bother to do a reality check on our values to see if they match with the organization. And although that may seem trite, it is the key to being happy at work.

We mistakenly think we are our title. We think we are the marketing manager, the CFO, the engineer, the production worker, or the human resource manager, but we are not. We give something much greater than that to an organization. It is impossible to give any less of yourself. You put forth eight to ten hours of your life, some eighty percent of your waking hours to this thing you call your job, away from your family, hobbies or artistic endeavors. Certainly, you give more than a set of skills.

You give your precious energy.

Some don't want to do anything in an interview but regurgitate skill. What drives that behavior is a deep fear of not being chosen. The need to be perfect and to have it together leads to the incessant need for approval. The need for approval is an endless well that will never be filled. It is not up to your employer to approve of you. It is up to them to *pay* you.

Isn't it odd that we ask questions about why a job is vacated, without asking about leadership? We never ask how they reward and define performance during an interview, either. We fear that questioning an employer would be the point of no return in the interview. The scales remain unbalanced; the employer holds all the power. Looking at the big picture, perhaps if we had expectations mapped out for us in the interview, we would be more successful after we accepted the job.

Over the years I could not help but chuckle at the similarities I saw between dating and the interview process. After you exit a failed relationship, you learn quickly that there is a game to be played, viable partners to meet and lifestyles to meld if you decide to re-couple. Unless you really understand the fullness of what you are about to sign up for when entering a person's life, you end up running from one failed relationship to another. To me it resembles the interview process and, sadly, most people's career paths. Asking questions up front and evaluating what you get out of it for the long haul is smart. No one manages your career anymore. It is up to you.

Do you think that if you understood how your prospective boss outlined his or her definition of performance, you would be able to hit the business targets? Do you think as a society, we would be more successful and spend less time trying to politic our way to the next pay scale?

Here is the magic.

Know thy values.

Know your values before you interview. Know what makes you happy. Know what is most important to you in an organization, and <u>then</u> find out if the organization matches your perspective!

Here are the definitions and examples of core values. Reflect on what is important to you.

<u>Core Values:</u>

Honesty	To consistently seek and speak the truth
	To have a business relationship without lying, cheating, stealing or other forms of deception
Respect	To value self, others, property and diversity
	To show appreciation for sacrifices that have been made for your benefit
	The ability to understand where your rights end and someone else's begin
	The ability to understand the boundaries of others and to establish boundaries with others to satisfy your needs

Responsibility	To be held accountable for your actions toward yourself, others and the company. To ask for forgiveness when you err
Individual Responsibility	To use good judgment and hold yourself accountable for your actions
Civic Responsibility	To have the motivation, knowledge and ability to actively participate in a communal society
Compassion	To show caring and kindness toward others and helping others who are in need
Courage	To face difficult situations with confidence and determination Standing up for one's convictions when conscience demands
Justice	To consider the perspective of others and to demonstrate the courage to be consistently fair To act impartial in the face of high emotions
Fairness	To treat people equally and make decisions without favoritism or prejudice
Teamwork	To become a productive and contributing member of a team To understand the importance of being a piece of the greater whole

Industriousness	To realize the intrinsic and extrinsic rewards of putting forth efforts to achieve personal goals

We forget. We forget who we are at our core. We do not demand that companies match our core values, and then are surprised when we hate our jobs. *It is not up to the company to make you happy.* It is up to <u>you</u> to make you happy, and to manage your career. No one else has those answers but you. Why would you ever hand your happiness over to a company, a person or a place? Handing over your power is downright dangerous and will only leave you feeling angry, rejected and confused. The power lies within you to choose the right employer, the right job, and to push your career to the next level or to decide that you are fine where you are. Either is a choice. Not choosing is a choice. But if you choose not to decide, do not blame your employer, the economy or your boss. It is your fault.

My assessment has been that the majority of us are not truthful and this stems either from a deep seeded fear of rejection, or a deep seeded need for everything to remain the same. Others are not truthful because they have not been in touch with that internal part of themselves for a long time. If you are willing to do the work upfront, this job hunt can be different. The end result is that you get a job that agrees with your skill set and values.

I realize that some of you may think I am on a soapbox, but I have seen what happens when a person is aligned with his or her values and looks for those values in a company. The difference in that approach to the job search is staggering in terms of the results achieved. This is far more than merely chasing a paycheck.

Here is an illustration of what I am talking about. Recently I began working with a client who had a real problem. It was more than just a job change. He knew he had to get another job because the one he had was killing him. Literally killing him. Emotionally he was a wreck, and it was starting to cause small health problems that would potentially escalate into bigger issues, like heart attacks and strokes.

He hated his job and went through much of the day feeling overwhelmed. Working for this company was like an endless fire drill. He knew how to complete the project, but he was not supported in the organization, and often found that he was the scapegoat in management meetings. If he could align with the people around him, he knew he could increase the company's profits. The people around him were not interested in collaboration and did not share his vision. They were ego invested and blamed each other for lack of progress. Sound familiar?

He knew what was coming and every night as he laid his head on the pillow, he fretted over his fear of being fired. He knew he had to get out of there and panic rose within him. Knowing something and doing something are two different things. He found that after a long day at the office, he was unable to muster up the energy to conduct a job search. His choices kept him in victim mentality.

Despite his exhaustion, eventually survival kicked in for him. The best friend anyone ever had is named pressure. He knew the company would not succeed and perhaps not survive the recession due to its poor leadership, and someplace inside him, he knew it wasn't his fault. It was like watching a train derail one car at a time knowing there was nothing he could do to stop it. Imagine going to work each day knowing that your company would fail and that there was nothing you could do to prevent it. He knew with hard, cold certainty that if they did not implement the next product line, then the local plant would shut down, jeopardizing not just his job but everyone else's too. It was a heavy burden on his mind, considering that he was responsible for twelve direct reports.

He found himself wondering how he could clean up this mess, for himself and his family. He just wanted to get out of his job and into another one. I warned him this was a dangerous place to be in. You never want to make career decisions under high pressure, or you are likely to find yourself working for a crazy boss for half the pay, kicking yourself in two months time for having taken the job. Fear makes you do stupid things. Caution at least enables you to slow down and think it through.

When I met him I was surprised to learn how far he had come in his career. After twenty years as a truck driver he returned to school at the ripe age of forty to study mechanical design. Upon graduating, in ten short years he worked his way up from drafter to engineering manager with an entire department under his leadership. He was a key member of the executive team and had a natural gift for orchestrating people and projects while keeping the business goals in mind. He was one of those people who liked to win, so seeing his current company in this state bothered him. One look at his resume clearly showed how much he would contribute to another organization if only he could find his way out. His positive attitude was infectious and his references were excellent, so I knew he would present well if given the chance to interview. Oddly enough, inside himself, he secretly worried that his skills were too diluted, lacking focus. He confided in me that he lay away awake at night, worrying 'they' would look behind the curtain and find nothing of real value. Of course, this was nonsense, but in the throes of a sleepless night, you can't tell a person that. Fear appears very real at three AM while you're staring at the ceiling.

The problem was not his hatred for his job or his impending layoff. The problem was that he had forgotten who he really was. Beaten down and lacking confidence, he thought his situation was who he was. He could no longer separate the situation from the learning experience. Disconnected, he was no longer aligned to who he was, or to his strengths and values. He found himself caught in the illusion.

I urged him to consider telling the truth at the next interview. Looking over his resume we saw that he tended to get stuck in organizations that were on their way down, instead of up. He longed to be picked and chosen by the employer, and because of that, he often forgot to ask the employer the hard questions to ensure it was right for him. He was seduced into accepting positions that were touted to be great, keeping his failure pattern going over and over again. I assessed that he was not appreciated for what he could really give to an organization, and he agreed.

Here was a person who had multiple talents, but did not have the confidence to abandon victim thinking and stand up for himself. Instead he stayed in survival mode. Within a year at each job, his responsibilities became blurred and he took on more and more, never asking for a raise or even a revised job title. Now nearing his mid fifties, he was tired, but not ready to slow down to a dead stop.

His drive compelled him to contribute at a high level, but the only way he could succeed was to tell the truth. The truth about what he was good at. The truth about what he was no longer willing to do. The truth about who he really was and what he had to offer to an organization.

This time he had to find a job that mirrored the truth of who he was, to marry both talent and his core values. Most of all, he had to have the strength not to accept less. Most people do not aim high and miss, instead they aim too low and hit.

There is nothing unique about this individual and I have done this work long enough to know that it can be overcome. First it takes honesty and awareness of oneself. Then, it becomes an exercise of being brave enough to tell the truth about who you are. And finally, it becomes about not accepting less.

The truth is a funny thing. It creeps up on you and cannot be squashed. Even if you are the master of avoidance, eventually life has a funny way of wearing you down, so that the truth comes up anyway.

Instead of just finding the next job, I suggest you take a long hard look at yourself, skill set aside, and think about what *really* makes you happy when it comes to work.

Be honest and ask yourself:

What am I really good at?

What parts of my job do I no longer want to do, or am I not good at?

Do I like the industry I'm working in?

Do I like my boss? Why or why not?

What are the three key values that are important to me at work? (Example: honesty, teamwork, communication)

Do my core values match the organization's?

Does the potential boss have these same values?

Do I feel appreciated, and at the end of the day do I feel that I accomplished something of value?

Looking over my resume, what was my favorite job? Why?

The least favorite job?

What are my marketable skills?

What is my talent?

Notice how the last two questions sound the same, but are very different.

Skill set equals money. For example, a Controller is paid between 80-100k, depending on the size of the organization and the list of responsibilities. However, *talent* equals the sum total of who you are. A Controller's talent may be in his leadership with his staff and his ability to retain people. It could be his ability to predict the future through building financial models and communicating the goals and pitfalls to the owners, so that the company is always successful.

Talent is that thing you do that no one else can do. It's that buzz inside of you when everything is clicking right along. It's when you work ten hours and don't feel tired after the commute. It is harder to measure, but if you look closely and are honest, it is there. I can always spot a client's talent and I focus on that, rather than getting caught up in the endless list of credentials on the page.

Telling the truth about who you are with the next employer is a matter of being honest and sitting down with yourself to ask the hard questions. Get a baseline and some tangible ideas about who you are and where you would like to go before you fill out the next job application online. Have a benchmark for what is acceptable to you this time around, and what is not. Start with your values.

After you know who you are, then you can be brave enough to ask the hard questions in an interview, and to uncover if it really is a 'match' for you. Consequently, it's an advantageous career move. I know how painful and frustrating it is to be stuck in a job that is no longer satisfying, but hear me when I say that slowing down to make the right next steps in your career will pay dividends. I've also been known to get caught up in the salary, rather than making sure the job fit my own personal values. The result was I took jobs that were more than I could manage and I ended up being miserable.

Consider the whole package—your skills, your talent and your values—prior to applying to any job online.

Chapter 3
Committing to Quit Your Job

Everyone considers leaving a job at some point.

As people, we want to be considered *responsible*. Society encourages us to be responsible, and rewards us accordingly. No one wants to be considered the type of person that bails out when the company gets tough and cutbacks are made. However, holding onto a dying system is not healthy (or profitable) either. Timing is everything. I have also witnessed people looking for a new job on Wednesday, rolling into the weekend and then thinking Monday will be better at work. Their efforts are inconsistent in the search and they remain unhappy, fooling themselves into thinking there is no place else to go.

Deciding can give you power and put your mind at ease. The most important point of power for any person is in the present moment and being decisive can release stress. For example, a good friend of mine was very unhappy in her job as a financial analyst for a major retail company. For months she agonized over staying versus leaving, not committing to either plan. We would talk for hours about her impending job search, but little action was taken. She read my first book, Recession Proof Yourself!, and called me full of excitement, exclaiming, "It's really this simple in life. Either you are staying or you are going. In fact, everything in life boils down to that statement. Relationships, jobs, places where you live. Either you are staying or you're going. Once you choose, life gets a whole lot simpler."

She made a good point. The key is decisiveness and committing to a decision. If you've survived the recession and kept your job, you will have to take some time to evaluate whether or not it makes sense to leave. Looking at upward advancement and the company's financials will tell you a lot. Sometimes the business relationship leaves you feeling so abused by all the extra work and hours you put in, you really cannot stay because you just don't have it in you any longer. After the layoffs happened, your job got bigger and so did your skill set. If you cannot be compensated for it, why not move on?

Staying or leaving can also be an issue regarding geographical location. Last week a client called me from Milwaukie, and had been in job search mode for eight months. Although employed, he knew that he needed to find another position as his company was in rapid decline. Due to the recession, the scarcity of jobs was another issue in Milwaukie. When another opportunity came to him from DC, he was faced with the decision of leaving the city where he had resided for nearly thirty years, and frankly it scared him. At fifty-seven, he knew the opportunity to relocate to DC was now or never. Clearly he was at the Y in the road and needed help weighing his options.

Fear is an indicator and actually holds an important purpose. The purpose is to protect you from something that may harm you bodily, mentally or emotionally. Distorted, it becomes a source of drama. People create their own hell through their thoughts. You are not your thoughts. You are not your job. You are not your ego. You are far greater and deeper than all of that.

To alleviate the fear and provide clarity, I created an exercise where we wrote down all the known and unknown facts for him to process, so he could choose if he wanted to move or stay in Milwaukie. Methodically, we concluded that relocation meant a new start, a larger city and good pay. Staying in Milwaukie meant the uncertainty of finding a job amidst high unemployment. I intuitively felt the move would enhance both his career and his marriage, but did not want to outright suggest it. Instead I suggested he get on a plane and check out the area to see if he and his wife found it suitable. Within a couple of days, a job offer came through and he took a bold step and accepted. Knowing this would change his life forever, he could no longer cling to what was not working. It was an act of bravery.

Regina and Ellie were no different either. They worked together in large nonprofit organizations in NY State. Each had been with the organization for more than 25 years when they saw the handwriting on the wall. A new CEO was instated seven years earlier and had done a good job of housecleaning the 'old timers' out the door. The CEO wanted the nonprofit to run more like a business and didn't value tenure. When both women figured out that the target was on their backs, I got the call. Imagine making a job change after more than twenty years. The stress, indecision and fear occupying a person can be monumental. Not knowing how to go about a job search, Ellie and Regina decided the fear of staying was far more dangerous than leaving.

Leaving a job after twenty-five years is a powerful decision. Like an abused spouse leaving a bad marriage, it often feels easier to stay and suffer. Choosing to leave is a courageous step into self-empowerment, and an act of taking care of yourself. It shows you are willing to change. It respectfully states the current situation isn't working for you any longer, even if you are unsure of exactly what you're diving into.

Others that remain noncommittal, claiming that no job is exactly 'right' for them, hold themselves hostage. Paralyzed, they sit at work and suffer. The longer you resist change, the scarier it is. It is a fear of the unknown that needs to be conquered.

I am no stranger to making hard choices, and the recession was unkind to me as well. Oddly enough, at the time these clients came into my life looking for direction, my own life eerily paralleled theirs. Residing in Oregon, with the highest unemployment rate in the nation, I found myself jobless when the firm I worked for went bankrupt. In fact, I was the last employee to turn out the lights and close the doors. The owner of the firm let me go with tears in his eyes because the bank would no longer float the payroll and there was nothing more he could do. Cleaning out my office was one thing, but when I returned a week later to give him back the office key, to my surprise I walked into a barren office. No desks or chairs remained. My boss was selling off the furniture to pay off his debts. It was hard to watch this man dissolve a business of fifteen years and to serve witness as all of his dreams and visions collapsed. This scenario didn't exactly fill me with optimism about my own life. With no severance and what I perceived as an old dusty resume, I was left to sort out my own life, no different than my clients. Although I could continue to build my consulting practice, I had to come to the hard realization that the business climate didn't need my expertise, and whatever money I could bring in wasn't enough to pay my bills.

My husband and I decided that it was best for both of our careers in the long run if we left the northwest for good. The hardest part of that decision was letting go and admitting that the path we were on would no longer work. Staying made the fight too hard. Resistance is like walking on broken glass, and I was tired of resisting. We both knew that finding another job in Oregon was not the solution. Overall, the economy was in shambles in our state and it was not going to get better. From my background I knew that we would repeat this same cycle in another ten years after the economy recovered. I refused to do that again. It made no sense for me to remain attached to a place where finding and keeping a job in my field was nothing but a struggle. As they say, you can't eat the scenery.

Both of our resumes showed a pattern of jobs held for three or four years, and each job change was due to our positions being eliminated or the company going out of business. It was never performance related. Oregon lacked a stable job market, and we were fortunate to be renting, so we had the option of walking away. It seemed the biggest issue was not just finding a job in Oregon, but trusting an employer with our financial stability, which clearly they could not promise. Retirement was my flinch point. I needed to know I could make a good living and start to save for our future. Although we resided in Portland, which is considered a large city, there were surprisingly few large companies to work for, leaving us with smaller employers in private companies. It is very stressful and difficult to build a life, sign for a mortgage or make any sort of financial commitment when you cannot guarantee your employment.

It was that day that we found ourselves in the middle of a should-we-stay-or-should-we-go scenario.

Strategically, we looked at relocation as an option. Keeping it in the fun space (mostly because I can be very serious), we explored three geographical regions that were excellent for both our skill sets. New York, San Francisco and Dallas topped our lists. Running relocation models online, it was clear that Dallas was the best financial choice with a twenty-five percent decrease in cost of living, as a bonus to us, as soon as we left Oregon. New York and San Francisco presented opportunities for high salary and income, but you'd have to be careful where you spent it in order to get ahead. The cost of living in both cities was higher, which made the reality of ever owning a home impossible.

Next, we took a hard look at what we did together, and what we really valued as a couple. Weekends, weather permitting, were devoted to taking long rides on our motorcycle. Twice a year, we took a ten-day trip, typically south, to enjoy the warm weather. Free time included looking at art, wine tasting and dining at great restaurants. We were not 'stay vacation' people. For us, weather was a factor in our choice of location. We both wanted out of the rainy state of Oregon, and took a hard look at what we loved to do. How we spent our free time told us a lot about what we valued as a couple. It became clear that New York was out. I could have moved there in a minute, but my husband would be a fish out of water and thrown into the desert. The long winters would limit our riding time, and frankly, the traffic made it a bit scary to fathom, tooling down the highway on a motorcycle. San Francisco, while very intriguing from my perspective, didn't offer much work fitting my husband's skills and industry background. The Bay Area was full of high tech and software companies; not an ideal choice for him. Also, it was unlikely we would ever buy a house in that market. While we could fund retirements more easily, which was a concern of mine, I had to come to grips with the hard fact that we would not have an asset called a home.

Close examination of myself revealed what my hard stop was, and ultimately it was three things: funding retirements, owning a home or some other large asset, and building a financial cushion for the next ten years. Interestingly enough, Steve's flinch point was insisting that we reside in a sunny climate, and that we had the ease of a large city where we could both find and retain steady employment. Together, we made some good progress in determining what we really wanted out of life, and discerning potential pitfalls.

To be honest, I was not enthusiastic about moving to the south and worried I would not resonate with the locals. Steve disagreed. Pressed to make his point, Steve looked at me and said, "If you took emotions out of it, the south allows us all that we are looking for. We can buy a house, get good jobs and fund retirements easily. We would extend our motorcycle riding to nine months of the year. For speaking events you could fly to either coast in three hours. It is centrally located. This could be a good ten year run."

That comment shifted me completely and I found myself ready to commit. He was right; it was a win-win for both of us. What stopped me was my preconceived notion of what life would look like in a city with which I was unfamiliar, and how I would fit into it. Fear of the unknown always stopped me in my tracks, and admitting that to myself gives me an added layer of empathy working with clients. I insisted on having data and making decisions based off facts, not feelings. Again I was ignoring my values and emotional well-being. I am no different than anyone else, and fear resides in me, though I try to make the right decisions. The point is that we were willing to let go of something that was clearly not working, and in this case it was our geography. The classic should I stay, or should I go question.

Relocation should be a careful choice a couple makes, if one is married. There is nothing worse than a trailing spouse leaving in support of the other person's dream, finding his or herself lost in a new city, unable to find their rhythm. In fact, that is a sure way to destroy a relationship. The move should be of value to both parties, otherwise, you don't go.

Staying or leaving is a personal decision and should be done with a strategic mindset and an evaluation of your heart. Take some time to sum up your feelings toward your company. Evaluate the pros and the cons of staying or leaving with eyes wide open.

Weigh the outcomes by asking yourself, "Am I paid fairly for my current skill set?" Pull some financial models and compare your skills to market worth. The easiest way to do this is to research your title and compare salaries to other organizations. The postings will outline the qualifications, duties and salary. Compare what you have to what you could get in the market. Often during recession, working Americans who survived layoffs are doing the work of two or three employees, making their skill sets larger; this could command more compensation if they went someplace else.

Audit your career by asking yourself:

Did the recession create more or less room for advancement?

Are you committed and happy in this job? Why or why not?

Is the company financially stable? Look at their financials over the last five years. What is the trend?

Do you trust your boss? Will s/he be an advocate and guide for your career path?

Will your boss leave the company? Does that change your picture?

Do you trust the leaders of the organization and believe in their decision-making?

If your pay was cut during the recession, is there a timeline to get it back?

If your health benefits and/or 401 (k) were cut, is there a timeline to get them back?

Deciding to leave a job does not equate to failure or giving up. Looking at the hard facts about your career and telling the truth will give you the answers. You have all the answers you need. They are all there, you just have to slow down, ask the questions, tune in and make a decision.

Knowing when the job is over and when to leave is where your power lies. Holding onto something with a cat's claws only makes letting go even tougher when the road disappears from under your feet. Surrender is the key. Letting go is being in flow.

Suffering is resistance to what is. Resistance to reality is painful. When your contingencies of what you need it to look like are outweighed by your inability to change, misery is the result.

Staying in a position with a company after recession may be a good choice for you. Certainly if you feel valued and you are compensated fairly, then stay.

Auditing your current employer both emotionally and financially is extremely valuable and can help you make the decision to start a job search.

When working for them isn't working for you anymore, it's time to leave.

Chapter 4
Fire Your Crazy Boss

Have you ever had a crazy boss?

The kind who asks you to do something, and after you deliver tells you they wanted something different. Two days later you complete that task and they claim they never gave you that instruction. Your productivity becomes a moving target, a game you will never win.

Or the type of boss who watches everything you do, constantly reinforcing their distrust of your ability to do the job correctly.

Or, my personal favorite; the clearly abusive one who plays mind games and makes you feel inadequate. The one that doesn't give you the tools to do your job, and sabotages you from the beginning, then blames you for not delivering. Weeks turn into months and they slowly chip away at any confidence you had in your abilities. They throw you under the bus, publicly, in emails and at meetings with your peers. They are big fans of public humiliation as a tactic to control and lead.

Ever have that experience in your career?

Susan Hauser's article in Workforce Management entitled, "The Degeneration of Decorum" discusses in depth the cost of civility (and lack thereof) in today's office environment. It turns out that four out of five employees experienced rudeness and hostility at work. Sixty three percent wasted time avoiding the offender and more than three quarters of respondents stated their commitment to their employer waned. A whopping twelve percent quit their jobs over lack of civility in the workplace. Clearly the leaders tolerated the behavior or caused it in some way. It is amazing that how one feels will color their depth of commitment and performance. Tolerating bad behavior in the workplace is as bad as causing it, and the leader sets the tone for standards and colors what is acceptable from team mates.

I would venture a guess that you have worked for a crazy boss a time or two in your life. Soon this experience will be a line item on your resume as you move on to bigger and better things. The hard reality is that most of us, at some point in our careers, have reported to someone difficult.

For whatever it's worth, I met with many of these hard charging leaders and was always shocked at how far up the ladder they got, despite their behavior. In three years I called on four thousand hiring managers and observed how they assembled their teams. I got a firsthand look at why a person is hired, fired and promoted. Quickly, I figured out how leadership is the make or break of any organization. Most leaders I met just wanted good production out of their people, and didn't have the faintest idea about how to go about getting that. The other unpleasant parallel I drew was that anything in their lives that was emotionally unresolved came out in the workplace daily.

For example, if they had a traumatic childhood and had trust issues, that surfaced in the team meetings. The office became a battleground where they relived old childhood wounds that caused them to act out and treat their staff poorly. As leaders, they could not be goal focused because they were not whole. These leaders would chew people up and spit them out. Employees refused to work with them and either left the company or got fired under their reign. However, these demanding leaders knew how to protect their own jobs, despite the abuse they cast on their staff.

Most leaders have no idea how much emotional trauma they cause for their direct reports, and I suspect that some of them would have changed their approach had they understood their emotional power and their ability to inflict such damage. Like a parasite and host relationship, it actually worked fine, until the employee figured it out and ran out the door, seeking relief from the abuse and hopefully bound for a better job.

Some leaders were simply detached. Overly logical, they forgot that *people* worked for them and not machines. Their workload expectations were better suited for robots. Regardless, it is difficult to work in a place where you have no connection with the person you report to. Trust is built upon time and consistency. Commitment to a company is more about a feeling than their financials.

Many of my clients suffered the reign of a tough leader. Their reactions went from being worn down at the end of the day to manifesting serious health issues due to the pressure they underwent at work.

A client of mine contacted me shortly after a triple bypass at the ripe age of fifty-three. The job contributed to his stress level, and now he had a lot of time in recovery to figure out what came next, realizing the obvious need for a different work environment. A job should never come before your health, although that is easy to say when you are not the one in pain. Many of my clients who worked for leaders they neither liked nor trusted were so anxious to leave that they rarely put any thought into where they would end up next. They just wanted out. They limped along in agony and were tired of it.

Happiness with leaders and direct reports often comes together when both parties share the same core values. If you both share values, trust is built. Together you accomplish more. Did you ever report to someone that you just clicked with? What did that feel like on any given day? A day at work becomes tireless because you multiplied your efforts with someone else that shared the same values.

It is possible that you can hire and fire people out of your life, including your boss. The choice is yours. This is the end of victimhood, and blaming others for what you don't like in your life. Don't like your boss? Find another.

Leah had a challenging situation with her job. She worked for a large health care corporation as a financial analyst when we met. Her job was very challenging and detail orientated. It took her six months to ramp up, but when she did, she was very successful. Most of her day was spent in Excel spreadsheets, poring over complex data. While the job itself was challenging, she was unhappy with her boss, and over time, developed concerns about how she was treated. It took her some time to realize it was neither the job nor the work itself, but the boss she reported to.

Mark had a habit of yelling at her over the cubes in the office, making her feel embarrassed. If a meeting agenda she created contained errors, everyone else would hear about it publicly in the meeting. Public humiliation was his power trip. Mark liked to give Leah partial information, and then complain that she was not doing her job. He set her up. Emails would have missing pieces, or she would be left out of the email chain completely, making her feel inept. Mark did a good job of making Leah feel like she was losing her mind, until one afternoon she meticulously backtracked through her inbox to confirm that she never received the email he was referring to after all. To add to this pressure, she would get direction from him and another woman in the office who was also known by her peers to be difficult to work with. Leah would do a task and then be told by this woman that she needed to do it differently or not at all. Her boss would step in from time to time and confuse the whole issue, making it impossible for Leah to produce quality work, because the direction constantly changed. For months, Leah was convinced the problem was her, but in reality it was the leadership.

Leah is the type of woman who internalizes things, mentally and emotionally, for a period of time before she reacts or responds. She is a thoughtful, quiet woman who likes to have all her facts in place before she speaks. She intuitively knew that her boss thought she was incompetent. Leah tried for months to overturn the perception, to no avail. In a fit of frustration, she even approached her boss and asked him to be mindful of his behavior. He denied anything happened, which made it clear to me that the situation was never going to change. He did not hold himself accountable for his actions. It was easier to pin it back on her.

Two points that were clear: Leah was not going to change and the leadership was not going to change. What would change over time was that Leah would find herself not wanting to be there, which is exactly what prompted her discussion with me.

This is the classic case of dealing with the crazy boss. You cannot win.

Parents can do this with children, and grown adults do this to their employees. For example, a child asks if they can go out and play. The mother responds no, because they need to do homework first. However, when the father is approached with the same request from the child, he answers yes. Getting the answer the child wants, he skips outside to play. Clearly the parents aren't on the same page or communicating well. The same sort of thing happens in organizations, which can lead to total pandemonium. When looking for another job, remember you get the *option* of interviewing them too. Go into the interview prepared; ask about the organization's overall goals, the company culture and how the leadership leads. Asking questions during the interview is not rude and it allows you to take back some control in the conversation. It keeps your eye on the ball and focused on the decision of whether this is the right organization for you. The only way to avoid a crazy boss is to ask the right questions.

The hiring process itself seems very ineffective if you think about it. You agree to devote the next several years to the company, giving them eight to ten hours a day for X amount of money, called your salary. The employer decides if you are worth X amount of money and if you will get along with the team.

Considering that eighty percent of your waking hours over the majority of your life are spent at this place called work, isn't it odd to make an important decision like this based on a total of two hours of conversations, otherwise known as the interview process?

But we do. That is our process, and it is inefficient and usually ineffective. We base our careers on this model.

The new model I propose is being proactive and recognizing red flags. Knowing who you are *first*, before you walk into an interview is an anchor. It will keep you grounded as you go about the interview, asking questions to uncover who they really are.

Look back at the values I listed earlier. The objective is to find an organization that aligns with **your** values. The bigger objective is to report to someone who has the same top three values that you have. Once matched, the job will no longer seem like a job. It will be magical.

The Core Values Are:
Honesty
Respect
Responsibility
Individual Responsibility
Civic Responsibility
Compassion
Courage
Justice
Fairness
Teamwork
Industriousness

As I write this book, it saddens me to report that I have only had two experiences in my entire career in which I felt great working for someone else, but I know these experiences made all the difference for me. Reporting to someone who was a fair leader and who got me was the recipe to staying in a job for a long period of time. Miserable, I moved from job to job, adding to my skill set and hoping for something better. But from the moment I met Wendy, I knew immediately that I could work with her.

There was something alive in her communication and judgment that made me see that work could actually be fun *and* I'd bring home a paycheck.

Through conversation, I found out she was from New York, and that made me feel at home.

I thought in the beginning that was our connection—through our tribe, but it did not take long to see that what we really had in common was three core values, those being: honesty, responsibility and justice.

I was one of Wendy's first direct reports, and she was astute enough to know she was transitioning into leadership. She knew she had to grow into the position with twelve direct reports, most of them being salespeople. Taking on a group of reports would be difficult for anyone, and then add to that the fact that they were high strung sales people in an agency. Frankly, Wendy was exactly what the firm needed. She knew how to sell, but more importantly, she knew how to be fair. She had a way with people, and taught them the value of sharing. Intuitively, she knew it would be the demise of the team if we fought against each other. She was also smart enough to know that she needed us far more than we needed her. Our sales were her merit of production.

Wendy was honest to a fault, if there is such a thing. I was never sure where that came from in her life, but she believed in being so honest that she would walk from a deal if it was not right for all parties involved; the client, the candidate and the firm. On a deep level, she needed to feel good about her work. Furthermore, she needed to go to bed at night knowing she had not ripped anybody off. Wendy needed honest money.

She believed in responsibility to others and she demanded it from her team. Her sense of justice came to light whenever we quarreled over a billing, wanting to get the fee for ourselves. Quickly, she would make a decision. She would turn to one of us and say, "You get the account. You did the work and earned it." To the other party she would say, "You get the next account. I'll make sure of it. Leave this one alone." Her decision being final, we would move on to the business of selling.

No one hated her for this, either. We respected her. We knew she had our interests in mind at all times. She was the type of boss who took on the organization and fought for you, leaving you to focus on your job. She was powerful enough to do that, and I doubt anyone ever saw how fortunate s/he was to have Wendy in his/her corner. I knew it clearly on the day she fought with the owner for my job.

It had been a tough year, and recession was in full swing. People were not exactly hiring headhunters for what they could do themselves. Billings were slim. The owner sat her down and went over the month's projections. He was an accountant originally, which only made matters worse. He looked at numbers and not at people.

While my billings were under by a hair, she made it clear; Elizabeth is untouchable. If you need to lay off others, do it, but not her. I will not work in this office without her. She is very valuable. She is our legacy employee, the very first one I hired. She builds relationships at a deep level, and none of her clients would ever move to the competition.

She was just. She did the fair thing. She knew what I had to offer and looked at a picture bigger than this month's billings. I did not have to politic and self promote because my performance stood.

She saw my efforts at the end of the day and was willing to fight for me. And in return, I was loyal, until the very end. Ultimately, a year later, the owner did lay me off and closed the entire firm. I was the last employee of twelve to go. Wendy had warned him for months that if I were to leave, she would follow.

It never occurred to me that what transpired could happen.

Within three weeks of my layoff, Wendy quit and went out on her own. She told the owner that she had made it clear for months that she would not work without me as her partner. With me gone, he left her no choice. The reality that she worked the business alone penetrated her each morning she opened the office in my absence. She figured if she had to do it alone, she would. But she would not do it alone and work for him.

Justice. A boss sticking up for you, doing right by you until the end. Frankly, that's who I want to work for!

This is a two way street. As Wendy's employee, I shared her values. I was that one employee who did not quibble over a deal. I was honest. If it was not mine, I did not take it.

I believed in fairness. I never gossiped about her or the owner behind their backs at lunch like everyone else did. While I never drew a hard line in the sand over my loyalty to them, everyone on the team knew where I stood. I decided in the beginning who I was going to be while working there, and controlled my perception as the friendly employee who was competent and caused no hassle for the management. I stayed true to myself. I openly embraced any changes management made that impacted me.

Furthermore, I was never angry and never had an outburst in the office. I became known as the rock, which amused me. Others speculated that I was the favorite, the 'untouchable'. Maybe I was. I paid little attention to what others thought of me and did my job, knowing next week they would pick on someone else. I remained friendly and professional with everyone at all times.

Wendy never had to ask me to do anything twice or to follow up. She was my boss, I respected her, and when she gave me something to do, I put it at the top of my list. I had an intuition about her, knowing what she would need before she asked. Together, we made money and laughter.

Wendy and I were successful in running the business by ourselves that last year, long after the others were fired or laid off. What made each day extremely pleasant was the fact that we shared the same core values. We never moved into competition with each other. We found that to be counterproductive. Our focus was holding the firm together and any emotion that did not align us with that goal was a distraction.

She was the first one to lend a hand if I needed help, although my pride insisted that I not ask until I was totally lost. She made it safe for me to bounce around ideas. I could go to her office, close the door from time to time and just talk about a bad day. She never repeated what I told her if I asked her not to. She honored confidentiality.

Wendy was the best boss I ever had. And it took me three whole years to realize she was the best because we had the same values.

Had the firm not closed, I would still be there. However, it was a blessing, because if I were still there today I would not be writing full-time, or speaking, or consulting. To end my headhunting career in the agency world with her was a wonderful transition into the next part of my life. Wendy gave me a gift by letting me go.

The key to success in business is being a good employee and constantly understanding the management. Notice the collaboration I had with my boss in the firm. Performing consistently, embracing change, being positive—all of those approaches—along with a solid leader that shared my core values made that job experience wonderful. You can have this too.

Consider who you work for as part of the total package of your job. Ask questions. Find out their values. Know yours.

Be brave enough to walk away from the offer if they do not align with you. It is ok to say no thank you and continue looking for the right job, with the right leader.

Chapter 5
Networking for Nerds

When faced with a job change, one can easily be trapped into thinking there is only one-way to find work. We believe that applying online is the only way to go. Not true. Studies have shown that shopping jobs online is not effective, and that most jobs are found through word of mouth or networking. According to Columbia University, 80% of jobs are found through a personal recommendation or personal referral.

Networking can be very difficult for the introvert, but it is a critical component of the job search.

I suggest that the job hunt be constructed in a tiered strategy.

Job seekers should network with others and construct a target list of 10 companies. Doing just one activity narrows possibilities. We want more options, not less.

Time plus consistency will always produce results and the job hunt is no different.

Think of the job search as *a process*. Each day you follow the process and then let it go of your attachments to results. You will find another job. Consider the process to be your compass through a maze called online postings.

Here is the process that I have given to many clients.

1) Go where you know. Meaning: look at online postings. We know there is an open job there. We know they are hiring. Put some energy into that activity, but know that you will also have competition as others will see the ad and apply.

2) Design a target list of ten to fifteen companies you would love to work for in the future. These are places you have heard good things about or you just love the product and technology. You have some level of interest for the organization. Do some preliminary work through research. Explore with the attitude of a detective trying to solve a mystery.

3) Network. The likelihood that you will be happy in a job that came from networking goes up dramatically. Networking is your point of power to find out the truth about a company. Networking works because you can

get an inside track into the organization. The possibility that someone could walk your resume into the hiring manager's office is a huge plus. Networking allows you to get candid feedback on how the company operates from a trusted source.

4)Build your LinkedIn. Connect with employees and business owners. You never know when an opening could pop up. Positioning is everything. You want to set the stage and be poised for the job so it can manifest. No one can be online constantly, and building your online network is another way to passively search to see what else is out there. When using LinkedIn you want a mix of those you know intimately in business, along with contacts you don't know as well. The downside of connecting with those you don't know well is that on a basic level people connect with people at the end of the day. Meaning, if they know you, it's familiar. Honestly, do you think there is a good chance if you connect with a stranger on LinkedIn they will remember you in sixty days if a position should materialize? Do you think they will remember your skill set? They may or may not. Overall, face-to-face networking is more effective, but there is still a small chance something may come of this activity. Consider joining groups to get a feel for the audience and members. Watch their online conversations. Bottom line: LinkedIn should not be used like your Facebook account.

Regardless of the activity, the most important exercise you can do is to manage and monitor your thoughts and your actions in the job search. Ensure they both align and, no matter how hard it gets, keep moving forward. Quantum physics reminds us that thoughts are energy. That energy collects and spins into motion. Showing up is most of the game. By that I mean show up to your job search. No one can do this but you. Before you know it, you will produce results.

Intention is the name of the game. Perpetually look at your thoughts related to the job search.

Prioritize where you spend your energy. Where your energy flows, your focus goes.

There are only so many hours in the day that you can job hunt. Schedule your time wisely, but most of all, be consistent. Don't let life get in the way of your job search. That is just another form of procrastination and distraction, which will take you further from your goal of getting another job. Consistent efforts will produce a result over time. Starting and stopping the job search will only leave you with a feeling of total frustration. Remember your commitment to leave your current position. It is a promise you made to yourself, so honor yourself by sticking to it. A good idea is to commit to setting aside a specific amount of time to get online and look at postings to see what is out there.

Explore networking opportunities. Try not to ride an emotional roller coaster with your current job. Instead go to work knowing that the time there will not be long. Adopt a position of being of service while you are still there.

Commit to the search and do not let life get in the way. Take some time each evening and skip having a beer and sitting on the couch. Have your spouse pick up the kids from soccer practice and while the house is quiet, get online and look. Start to live in the realm of what is possible and out there for you. Many of us waste time online looking at articles and answering emails. Instead, make the search the priority. I cannot emphasize this enough; consistency is key. The worst thing I can imagine is that you miss a good job opportunity because you were not paying attention.

Consider confidentially reaching out to your personal network by email and placing phone calls to let them know that you are looking for another job. This is your built in network. Leverage it because the people in that network are there to help you. Before you ask, be clear in what you are looking for and be able to articulate that. You just never know where the next job will come from, and leaning on your network is an easy way to find a good position.

We are all connected in life. Others will help you.

Knowing not only what you have in your current job, but really knowing what you want in your next job is powerful. Clarity is critical when networking.

Tell your family and friends that you want another job. Tell them what you would like to do next. Think out loud. This is the easiest type of networking because you know them. They will hold your dreams, secrets and visions in their hearts until you step into the reality. Even if the new job does not come from them, just talking about it out loud will make the transition feel real. After creating your target list, take the top three and ask others if they know of any open positions at those companies. You just never know.

They might. Suddenly your resume is hand walked into the manager and there you are! Perfectly positioned!

Or not…it doesn't really matter. The point is to create energy and movement around what you really want in your life as you discover ways to find it. Life is like a treasure hunt without a map. You never know where the job will come from, and looking with an adventurous eye is more fun than churning out endless online applications. You will feel in power and in control if you follow this simple prescription: Always keep connecting the dots. Everyone and everything is connected. Where do you fit in?

Some job seekers have no idea where to start when networking, and wake up one day realizing they have no network. The easiest way to expand your network is to meet others in your field. Check your community to see if there are any professional meetings relevant to your line of work and make room for them in your calendar. Yes, I understand you may not get home until nine PM exhausted from a long day of work. But aren't you willing to give up one evening to free yourself from the agony of your current position?

People get anxious in networking situations because they feel that it is rude to ask a total stranger for something. Many have shared with me that networking feels like a sales job in which they are ill equipped. The smoother and more comfortable you are with yourself, the easier these conversations will be. When speaking to a total stranger in a networking capacity, all you have to know is who you are, what you do and the type of position you want. Breathe. Relax. Tell me who you are and where you'd like to go.

Still getting cold feet just thinking about networking?

I have worked with introverted clients who needed coaching on this very subject. The mere thought of going into a crowded room and networking made them break into a cold sweat. Some shared with me that the exercise itself was a waste of time. If networking is uncomfortable for you, here is a strategy that you can implement.

Consider arriving at a networking meeting a few minutes early and picking a good seat. Take a breath. Look around and notice who is seated next to you. Start the conversation by saying, "Hi, I'm Jill. I work at XYZ Company as a project manager. What do you do?" Then smile at them.

This is the easiest way to break the ice when you are the new kid on the block.

Listen to the response of the person next to you that answered your question. Listen with your mind, heart and ears. Try not to judge or think ahead about what they are saying, even though you still may be nervous. Then, if appropriate disclose something more about yourself by saying, "Well actually, I'm confidentially looking for another job in manufacturing. In fact, I'm trying to get into a few companies lately through networking. I'm very interested in Nokia and Intel." Stop speaking. Listen to their response. Do they know anyone there?

If appropriate, dig a little further and ask, "Would you know anyone there I could talk to? I was curious about the company culture and what they are really about. While their job postings look great, I'd really like to meet someone who works there."

See how easy that was? You just planted a seed. It's not sale-sy and it's not impolite. It's direct.

This small, brave act is more about full disclosure. Stop the lie your mind tells you, the one that makes you afraid to find another job. The lie that tells you that you are separated and alone. The lie that tells you how awful networking can be.

Speaking from experience, I remember how hard it was for me to re-build my entire network in Dallas after we relocated. For more than a decade I had worked and lived on the West Coast, and now found myself knowing no one, unable to articulate what I did, and I felt less than confident in my abilities. I forgot who I was at my core. What I did for over a decade didn't matter anymore because no one in Dallas knew me.

Confused, I wasn't even sure which networking groups to join, because the city was so large and offered so many different meetings. The danger was not the lack of networking opportunities, but the difficulty of finding the right group with the right audience that would hire me or even need my services.

Fortuitously, within a month, I only knew three people, but those three people pointed me to the right groups. And, I was lucky to be invited into the group and to the meetings. One rainy night, scared out of my mind, I drove with the GPS to downtown Dallas, hoping I could find the large hotel where the mixer was held. I found it, and it ended up turning into my first speaking engagement to the Texas A &M Alumni group, which was a fabulous opportunity.

You will never find what you are looking for sitting in your living room.

Many clients I've had think they have nothing to offer another. That is simply not true.

Remember, networking is about connecting and sharing information. Offer the person your network after you ask them to open up theirs. Ask if there are any contacts that they may need, and offer an introduction. It's about sticking together in this thing we call the job search.

Yes, everyone is unhappy. Yes, everyone wants another job. Together, if we share information and stop focusing on our own agendas, we can get to where we are headed.

The definition of networking is an interconnected system of things or people. It is the interconnection that will help bring your new job into reality.

Networking should be an exchange of positive, valuable information. It should not be engaged in with the intention of using others or producing a result. Instead, consider networking another opportunity to plant seeds. What you sow, you will reap.

People are connected to people.

Get into the flow and the movement of life!

Chapter 6
Click, Upload, Send, Wait

Applying online to what you deem to be the perfect job posting and not hearing back can be frustrating and discouraging.

There are a number of reasons why job seekers encounter obstacles when applying online. Think of it from the employer's perspective. By the time a job is open, something happened, and there are only three scenarios. Someone quit, someone was fired or someone went on maternity leave and never came back.

Occasionally, in a robust economy a fourth scenario plays out, which is, the workload went up and they need to add another person. During a recovering economy, such as the one we are facing as our country rebuilds, this is possible. Regardless of which scenario, this situation triggers the manager to walk down to the Human Resource Department and proclaim, "Sally just quit. Run an ad and let's see what we get. If anyone is good, email their resume to me."

The Human Resource Manager, in an effort to be compliant and helpful, posts the ad, hoping to attract the 'perfect' (notice the quotes) candidate for the manager. Remember that recruiting is not the Human Resource Manager's only job. HR has payroll to run, benefits to keep track of and employee relations, among other time sensitive projects.

What you don't know is that the ad you found online was constructed from a job description written five years ago when the last person quit. And, if that doesn't make it complex enough, the manager who ran that department retired three years ago. What you read is a pile of words that people who are no longer there wrote. The ad that Human Resources is posting right now on Monster.com and Craig's List is not what is needed in the job today, and does not fit this manager's picture of the 'perfect candidate'.

Roll the tape forward to you.

You are at your current job and on your computer with a cup of coffee and applying to a job posting that was written five years ago by a manager who is no longer with the company. You have no idea all this is happening as you hit the send key and read the automated response stating that your email was in fact received and thanking you for your application. However, if you are lucky enough to get a call inviting you to interview, you will quickly figure out that no one in the conference room really knows what skills they want for the job at hand. It's like looking for an opening in a dark cave when all you have is a Bic lighter.

The job search wears on for weeks as you sit in your cube at lunchtime with a half-eaten sandwich in front of you wondering if anybody out there in cyberspace is reading your resume. There is nothing but dead air, and the silence is deafening. You feel tired, frustrated and fear that you will never get out of your current job, which by now has become a living hell.

None of this is insurmountable. The truth is every job out there has what I call a margin of error. The margin is only as big as you make it by not asking questions. Give the employer a break.

More times than not, they are fishing for the right person and do not know what they really want. Few managers can fully articulate what they need in terms of skill set and personality. Furthermore, few can describe their company culture. Realize that what you're dealing with is a loosely written job description. Be prepared to ask detailed questions in the interview to uncover what they really need. Determine if you are qualified, where you are light or heavy for the position at hand, and if you are willing to do the job.

Remember, this time is different and your job search strategy is different. The objective is to get a good job in a highly functional organization. You already have outlined who you are and what you will and will not put up with, and are comfortable articulating that in a professional manner. But in an interview it is critical to ask questions that will uncover _who they are_, and then make the decision if you want to work there or not. This means you own your power.

Ask the hard questions such as:

Why is the position open?

If it is newly created, that is great! You have a chance to pave your own way and really give your talents to the job. The hiring manager will not know the difference because there is no benchmark with which to measure your performance in terms of who had been in the chair last. In this scenario, you have no place to go but up.

What types of people are successful here?

Reviewing your core values, see if they match. Knowing ahead of time who gets promoted and why is extremely valuable. No manager is going to come out and say that all promotions are done politically and made by random selection, but you can at least ask the question.

What types of people are *unsuccessful* here? Why is that?

Find out why Bob was fired last quarter and if you can have his office. Believe me; a manager will start to give you the tick list of what they do not like. During an interview you are there to ask, listen and solve their problem. Information is power and now you have some. You have choice in this, too. It is not all about the employer picking you for the job. Review the responses and decide if you want to sign up for this or not.

During the recession, business was affected. How did this organization get through it and where do you think you are going from here as a company?

Ah, the perfect state-the-obvious-and-go-into-the-future question. This question will flush out financial plans that haven't been thought through. Is the employer worried about quarter-to-quarter earnings, or the next three years? It will also tell you what type of leader you have in front of you and if they bother to think ahead at all. Frankly, their ability to look further out than next quarter will affect you and your job if you report to them.

What are your expectations for the first ninety days?

This gives you the roadmap of the expectations. *If they cannot answer this question run!* Abort mission immediately. Something is dreadfully wrong. You already have a job you do not want. The point of the exercise is not to go produce the same crappy job or crappy boss!

What is the formal review process?

This is a perfectly reasonable question. Now we are talking about performance and reward. If the company has no formal review process, or you are expected to write your own review (which is not uncommon in big companies today), that is something you should know about upfront. Review processes that are just reviews without bonuses, cost of living increases or merit raises based on performances are just that—reviews on performance. Which means get your money up front in your salary because it could be some time before you see an increase. That is acceptable, just find out upfront.

Describe your leadership style.

Expect them to lie. Most will. Do not be surprised if the manager's jaw drops when you ask this. Some may not be able to articulate what their style is in leadership. But ask. At least you threw it out there and may come away with some idea of how they like to work with others.

What are the three most important skills you are looking for in this position to be successful?

They should be able to answer that with no difficulty. Only ask if you want the job, otherwise, it does not matter and the question comes off as insincere. After you ask, reinforce that you have those skills, relating to stories that happened in your past jobs so they can make the parallels of who you are to the job that is open.

Finally, if you are interested in the job, ask them, "When do you intend on making a decision? " This is called a soft close and cues the audience that you are interested. Basically, you are poking around when things will happen and if you are the right candidate for them. It's okay to tip your hand and let them know that you are looking at other opportunities. Human nature wants what it cannot have, so stating that you are looking elsewhere only makes the interviewer want you more.

Narrow the gap in the margin of error, by asking questions and listening to their responses. Take your power back by being present in the conversation! Consider their entire response including body language, eye contact, shifting in a chair, anything that will point to who they are outside of the words that come out of their mouths.

Remember, we are not signing up for a crazy boss again, right?

Despite all of our best efforts, sometimes you apply online and never hear back. This happens for a variety of reasons. The most common is that the audience (HR) doesn't understand your resume or what you do. When this occurs, all you know is you didn't get a response, but actually, this behavior points to a poor internal hiring process within the organization.

These are organizations that are only as good as their hiring team. When the market is tight and there are fewer jobs available, Human Resources gets bombarded with hundreds of resumes, each one screaming at them (or begging) that they are qualified. Overwhelmed, they choose the top fifty off the printer and go with those, throwing the others out. If you are on the bottom of the pile or they don't understand what you do, you didn't make the cut. The best way around that obstacle is to make it painfully clear that you are **THE** person for the job through your resume.

Make it easy for the reader. Show them the common points between their job posting and your resume. Make the titles match, too, which makes it clear that you have done the job before. Titles can be deceiving. Go with what language they know for the initial resume. You would be surprised how your whole world will turn around if you make it very clear that you have mastered the hands-on required skills for the job. Having accomplishment statements are great, and personally I love them, but often readers miss the connection. They want to be secure and comforted that you know how to do the daily tasks. Weave both into the resume, but bubble their most important skill sets (which you will find on the ad) in the top.

If you remember nothing else in this chapter, remember that what you put out there into cyberspace is important. If you are not getting calls on your resume, you are not resonating with the reader.

In the world of online applications, it's easy to forget that you are actually applying for a job and a person will be reading your resume. Your resume should be written in a perspective and format that is helpful for them to understand what you have to offer.

While the process of applying online seems mechanical, it is not. It's about a person receiving your resume.

The final and most important step to applying online is following up. While I realize this can be a pain, it is the most important step you can take in the job search. Like losing ten pounds, you would have to commit to a regimen of diet and exercise. Finding a job means applying online and following up. Make sure not to get caught in the online maze. Take a bold step; get the manager's name, put a call in and ask if they received your resume.

You would be surprised how knowing where you stand can make you feel a lot better. Do not ask for an interview or sell yourself on the phone, but instead hold their feet to the fire and simply ask if they got your resume. If you hear someone on the other end of the phone searching through mountains of paper on their desk, that is a good sign, at least they know you are there and you cared enough to follow up. Do not, if you can help it, call on HR to ask about your resume. Find the hiring manager and let them know you did go through the proper channels of applying online but wanted to ensure that they got it. It shows your sincere interest in the company and also tips them to your work ethic. Besides, the other six hundred people who applied online are not doing this, which will automatically knock them a few pegs lower. By showing up, you'll get attention.

With LinkedIn, it is pretty easy to find a manager's name. The phone directory will give you the main number. Put a call in when the manager is most likely to be at their desk at nine AM or at two pm. Give people time to get a cup of coffee and sort through the first few emails. Statistically, people are likely to be at their desks during those times. Do not feel funny about calling them.

I promise they will not hang up on you or yell at you. All you are asking is for a professional response to the question about getting your resume. No one has ever died by putting in a call like that. And, as you will find in time, most people are pretty nice. They know you are in job search mode and once or twice before they have been in that mode themselves. Surely, they will answer you.

Track all of your progress on an Excel spreadsheet. It is very important to know where you went and if/when you got a response, because over time you will see a pattern. The tracking sheet will give you data and facts. Within sixty days you will quickly understand a trend of industries that are hiring, how many positions are available in your field and some ballpark figure of what they pay. The job search tracking sheet should have several columns including the name of the employer, how you found the job, their full contact information and lastly the result of what happened. Capture the result about the process and notate if you got a phone screen, interview, offer or rejection.

Rejections tell you something. Consider them to be data with a logical mind, knowing that rejections are not a personal attack on your career or your character.

If you do follow up after you have been rejected, ask for feedback in terms of why you were not considered. Only then can you work toward turning around the perception of your interview and hone your style. Remember it is an interview. It should be balanced with your questions in mind, too.

Eighty percent of life is just showing up. But you have to show up for more than just a mouse click. It is too easy to hide behind the blue glowing screen.

Becoming a person instead of a piece of paper allows you to be seen and heard. And believe it or not, managers hire people, not the paper. The resume is a small step in getting invited to interview, to open the dialog and explore your candidacy. Interviews are invitations. Following up will make you feel in control of your job search as opposed to applying online and waiting endlessly for the call.

It is no fun waiting around hoping to be picked like some puppy in a pound.

Walk out of cyberspace and into real life.

Chapter 7
Clever Cover Letters That Get Read

A common misunderstanding my clients have is how much information should be on the resume. For some, they think the resume should be a place to prove all the reasons they are a good fit for the position. Others are so overwhelmed by the cover letter assignment that after looking at a blank screen for hours, they re-write a summary of their resume. Numerous books and articles have been written on this topic, with much debate about what is the 'right' approach.

The first thing to consider is who is receiving your cover letter. More than likely, you are applying online and it will go into the inbox of a Human Resources person on the other end of the desk. This person may be a senior leader with years of experience or a junior employee hired to screen you out. If you are very lucky, a hiring manager will read your letter, but more likely, if you are fortunate, your information will be forwarded.

Regardless, it is safe to assume—always—that HR will be the first set of eyes on your cover letter and information. They are not specialists in skill set. They are _generalists_. Recruiting is not even the most important function of their job, so keep that in mind and be gentle with them. Do not bore them. Most importantly, remember you are one of many in their email box, wanting an opportunity to speak to them about this job. Polite and respectful is the approach.

As a recruiter I received thousands of cover letters, most of them missing the correct approach with me entirely. The cover letter I remember the most was the one that was unusual. I distinctly remember that he sincerely thanked me for my time, acknowledging that he was the only person vying for my attention. He knew I was busy and treated me with respect. He ended the letter with a compliment on my abilities and my organization. I called him immediately, thinking that this was the type of candidate I wanted to know more about, and a simple email would not do. I wanted to hear his voice and meet him. I wanted the conversation beyond email. Frankly, his hook worked!

How do you think you can get a reader motivated?

Think about the point of the cover letter. The only point of the cover letter is to keep the reader interested enough to double click and open to your resume, where you will be judged. It is a page-turner. The best approach is to be pleasant, somewhat informative and very concise.

For years I have been asked to author cover letters and explain why my version tended to work. Here are two examples of cover letters that work:

Cover Letter Sample #1

Please note this goes into the body of the email itself, not as an attachment.

Hello,

Thank you for taking time out of your busy day to read my resume.

I noticed you had an ad for a (insert job title here), and wanted to reach out to you directly. Currently I am working and looking at very select opportunities. Frankly, your ad caught my attention due to your company's product line and core values.

Looking at your online posting, my relevant experience can be found during my tenure at (enter the last company where you worked where this is relevant)

Perhaps my background in (add a broad skill statement here) would be of value to you. At this point in my career, I'm looking for an organization that values its employees, where I can contribute immediately and be a respected team member.

I'll leave this in your capable hands and thank you for your consideration.

Best Regards,

Enter Your Name Here

Re-read the cover letter again carefully and I will explain in detail why this works.

First, the letter acknowledges the reader and the fact that s/he is busy. That is considerate and polite. Furthermore, it shows that the letter is not all about the job applicant. It is focused on the reader. Most HR people get cover letters that have a needy tone to them, asking or begging for a job. Others start in an informative, arrogant tone. The cover letter is different in that the opening tone considers the reader. It also draws the reader into the content in the next paragraph.

Furthermore, it states that this particular candidate is working. People want what they cannot have. An employed candidate is a highly desirable candidate from the employer's perspective. It gives them an opportunity to steal you away from your current employer. It also paints the picture that your skills are current and you are not on the government dole, unlike other candidates that may apply. Top talent is always working, making the reader more enticed.

The next paragraph sums up which position the job seeker is interested in, just in case there are multiple openings in the company. It clearly tells the reader where to look for the related job skills that correspond to the job posting. You just made HR's job easier, and they are thankful. Then it goes on to compliment the organization and show that the author of the cover letter did some preliminary research on the company based on its comments about the organization's values. Everyone loves the person who did his or her homework! Clearly this individual did, and it makes the reader want to read on.

While this paragraph says very little about the actual skills that the author possesses, that alone makes the reader want to double click on the resume. Saying less is really more in this case. It quickly states they have some skills, but makes you go to the actual resume to find the facts.

The last paragraph pushes the reader into their ego, emphasizing that they trust they do their job well, and may even choose to pass them along to the hiring manager. It is a classy way to close a cover letter, and frankly, it works.

Cover Letter Sample 2

Hello,

Thank you for taking time out of your busy day to read my resume. I'm certain you'll get a lot of responses to your ad.

I am writing in response to your (insert position title here), in the hopes of exploring this opportunity with you. I have heard good things about your organization, specifically how you are the leader in (enter some fact here) and believe in (enter a company core value here). At this stage in my career, I'm looking for an organization that supports the growth of their employees, and a place where I can contribute at a high level immediately. Currently, I am a working candidate looking at selective opportunities.

Perhaps my background in (enter two broad skill sets that are requirements on the job description here) would be of value to you.

Sincere thanks for your consideration.

When the time is right for you, please give me a call.

Best Regards,

Your Name Here

This is a slightly different approach, but offers the same result. The reader will be enticed to double click on your resume.

Look at the first paragraph. The tone is friendly and thankful to the reader. Like it or not, the reader has all the power to get your information onto the right person's desk, or to make the decision of whether to call you or not. Stating that you know they will get a lot of ad response lets them know you think they are a desirable organization. Everyone likes that. Everyone wants to work in a popular place. It feels good. And it is even more fun if you are on the inside, looking at others who want to be where you are.

Paragraph two outlines the job the author is applying for and states that they know something about the company, which gives them automatic bonus points. Again, notice the cover letter is not about the author; it is all about the reader, taking into consideration how they may feel.

The next paragraph is a teaser about the author's skill set. If you want more, you will have to see the resume.

The close is the most powerful. It simply says, when the time is right, please call me. It gives the reader the power and paints the picture that the author is not sitting around hoping their cell phone will ring. The tone relays that the author is busy, the reader is busy and that s/he hopes they can connect. Again, people want what they cannot have, and although the close is professional, it does not lend itself to a needy message.

Cover letters are tricky but do not underestimate their power. This is a game of double click. We want to motivate them to click on your resume.

Remember: There is a real live person on the other end of the computer screen reading your information.

Chapter 8

Social Media, Friends and Tweets

In October of Two Thousands Nine I did a webinar called "Snoopy Employers" that got national attention. Apparently it struck a chord. Featured stories were subsequently written about me and about the secrets I disclosed, hoping to arm candidates with facts on how an employer thinks when they snoop around at your online profile.

We are all fooled by the power of online perception. I have been quoted to say that what stays in Vegas ends up on U Tube, Twitter and your 'friends' Facebook page and I stand by that statement. Many a candidate has been screened out due to their brash bragging of partying too much over the weekend or taking home a stranger. Mostly, it is Gen Y that suffers from not getting the job due to ignorance that only youth can provide. Think of it from my perspective as an employer. After a quick Google search, I know if you dabbled in pot smoking a week ago and will fail the drug screen. I know your political views, which do not match mine, which may inflame me because you openly talked about it through some clever little slogan you posted on your wall. Furthermore, I now read way too much about your sex life. No employer wants to know such things about their potential employee. And frankly, an online rant of your last weekend with recreational drug and alcohol use only makes you a high-risk employee. We instantly judge and doubt your ability to perform the work on Monday morning, not to mention that you are a possible a risk for our health insurance policy, of which, by the way, we pay half. Furthermore, we weed you out after three minutes upon viewing your U Tube video. We got a real intimate look at your Facebook page and can sum up who your real 'friends' are outside of the water cooler.

The other issue with Facebook is that your personal hobbies are out for everyone to view. For example, I am a writer and have a radio show. I've conducted seminars and private executive coaching for individuals and groups for more than a decade. For years, this was all in addition to my day job. When potential employers met me they would ask about my practice, fearing that I would not dedicate a full week to them or would balk at overtime. Often in interviews I would have to explain that these were all things that I did on the side, and actually complimented a potential employer on a variety of levels.

However, it was clear that if anyone Googled my name, my LinkedIn, Facebook and Twitter pages would come up, and lead them to conclusions. Suddenly I had to explain and control my online perception.

Jeremy, my editor, faced the same sort of questions in an interview. Jeremy is a talented writer and actor, which is where his joy resides. Yes, he has a day job, but nights and weekends are spent with the artistic crowd where he can continue to grow his creative side. An educated engineer, this man finds his balance in expressing himself through plays. Employers will ask him skeptically in an interview after pursing his Facebook page, "I see you are also an actor. How can I be assured that you will dedicate time to this position? Do you have plans of moving to Hollywood and pursuing acting full-time?"

I can already hear readers start to stamp their feet and tell me that it is their Constitutional Right and that they have Freedom of Speech. It is their God given right in this country to say and write anything they want online.

You are correct. It is your right. Go right ahead.

We will not hire you.

Ever!

Not in one million years.

I'm very busy and very sorry but next candidate, please!

Employers are not looking for what you say in an interview, but rather *what you do*. Your online proclamation is a declaration of your character. Look to a person's behavior to know what they are really about. People's actions will give you all the data you need about who they really are and where you stand. While it may be hurtful and disappointing discovering who someone really is, from an employer's perspective your online posts paint a picture of who you are outside of work, and they want to know.

Let me warn you about what really happens in the hiring process. This is what a real day in the life looks like as a person on the other side of the desk receiving your resume.

It's Thursday morning and your email just hit my inbox with your resume attached. It looks nice enough. Good, legible font. Pleasant enough cover letter. I print it out and pull the two pages off the printer only to return to my desk and type GOOGLE into the search box. Up pop corresponding links to your LinkedIn, Facebook page and a Twitter account.

Most of us are familiar with social media, but for those that aren't, let me explain. Facebook is basically an online profile of a person, usually depicting family pictures and 'friends'. Note that <u>anyone</u> can be a friend. Readers beware that there can be online pictures of people the author has never met before in real life. They may be cyber friends and not real people in their day-to-day life. Facebook uses the term 'friend' loosely. That's ok in this space (not My Space) we call them 'friends' but don't be fooled. As employers, over our morning coffee we will read in graphic detail your online life and look for suspect weekend behavior, songs you like, artists you hate and your upcoming plans with your sister-in-law for Thanksgiving dinner.

I think that pretty much covers Facebook. It is casual backyard BBQ talk, but it's interesting nonetheless for an employer to read. Conversely, if you are mid-level career, you'll bore us to death with pictures of your perfect grandchildren and trip to the Grand Canyon last summer. My husband calls Facebook narcissistic because everyone lies about how great their life is, when actually they are miserable. His theory is it's a place to publicly make yourself out to be much larger than you are, where you flaunt the illusion of a glamorous life to your siblings. Your adult kids are better, your backyard is better, your grandchildren are better, the weather where you live is better—basically, you have the life and uh, they don't. Welcome to Facebook. Keep your ego engaged and hold onto your hats, because these people you 'talk' to will not be the same people you see at the family reunion. For there they cannot hide the discontent in their lives, but on Facebook, well, everything is rosy! Note: the employer who sees your page does not know any of this.

Twitter, however, is much different. Twitter allows you to gather 'followers' which again, are typically people no one knows. For example, I am a "follower" of Kevin Spacey. I've never met him, but like his movies, especially American Beauty. Yet, I digress. Twitter allows people to send out "Tweets" to their "followers". In my example of Kevin Spacey I keep hoping he will send out a Tweet that he has a good movie coming out. I'm still waiting. He doesn't seem to Tweet very much these days. Twitter got a lot of press after a man did a shout out on the website proclaiming a plane had crashed into the Hudson River—before the press could get the news out on the wire. As Hiring Managers and Recruiters, we are looking at Twitter and reading your Tweets. Most of them are boring, but we will read them anyway. We are also interested in who you are following. Birds of a feather stick together, right?

LinkedIn is the most powerful online tool out there right now in the workplace. It is the showboat of who's-who in the white-collar world. When I was recruiting, typically I cut to the chase and went there. Within three minutes (and that is all we usually take to read your profile), I know your skill set, your interests, your industry and perhaps even see a picture of you. While I could read the resumes on my desk with the coffee cup ring on it, LinkedIn allows me to also see your 'connections', your background, what city you live in and, if I'm lucky, a headshot.

These online tools quickly give an employer, recruiter or hiring manager all they need to know before you even walk in the door to interview. It is common knowledge that most companies, large and small, will actually screen out candidates before the interview by getting online and reading what you are up to in your personal life. Used as a screening tool to get you out of the running, an employer is not going to tie up time and effort in salaries, drug testing and background checks if in clear print we know that you cannot pass. This knowledge also points to your future behavior. Or possible future behavior, I should state. The thinking is if you smoke pot or drink now, is there an addiction brewing? Why should we as employers sign up for that? We want employees who show up on time, ready to work, and care about the work they do for eight hours for us.

All I can advise for you as the candidate is control your persona. Online marketing is just that. It paints a picture of who you are and what you do on your off time. I always suggest that a person clean up their online persona before they send out resumes to a company.

I think we are also fooled into thinking that people we spot on LinkedIn are potential contacts for us to network with during the job search. It is poor form to try to connect online with someone you don't know and pick them for information that serves you. Most people will not even respond to your request, nor should they. This is hard for very technical people to understand when they build relationships online, but business relationships are different. They should be done in person with a handshake, just like in nineteen-eighty.

After a recent webinar I hosted, a participant asked me what he should do when a stranger invited him to connect on LinkedIn. I told him that while I do have over three hundred contacts in my LinkedIn, I actually know all of them personally. Most were employees of large companies whom I did business with for years. Some were old clients who enjoyed following the progression of my writing and speaking career as it unfolded.

People would see my online profile and want to connect with me, hoping that I could introduce them to others, so they could benefit from my various contacts. When approached by people I didn't know, I wrote a polite, professional email stating that my LinkedIn contained close business contacts of mine and that I did not let just anyone in my little black book. Most took that gracefully. Other times I just shot them a note asking, "Do I know you?"

Another sticky situation that comes up is when a coworker asks you for a recommendation on LinkedIn, and you do not feel comfortable giving one. Their only way out is through. Just be polite, tell the truth and let them know you are uncomfortable. A couple of years ago, a business acquaintance asked me for a recommendation. Personally, I found her to be pushy, and in all honesty I could not recommend her. The only way I could get out of her request was to tell the truth. I could not honestly comment on how she conducted business. I never did business with her. We were merely colleagues, thus I told her I couldn't recommend her. She got the message: Stop leveraging my reputation to get you someplace. Go build your own.

And, let me tell you, all employers know how it works anyway. You stroll down to your buddy's cube and ask for the write-up and post it on LinkedIn. We all know when we read a recommendation that isn't accurate. Frankly, I would rather call your references and drill down.

Recently a reporter emailed me asking why on earth people post things online after all the articles have been produced on the dangers of social media. My response was that you are likely to see more shocking statements online from Generation Y than of older generations. For them, this is just a post or just a 'friend' they are talking to online. They grew up with technology, online video games and texting. They grew up thinking that typing someone's name meant there was a relationship. They grew up thinking that face-to-face conversations were not real, but stuff that happened online was real. You will also notice they have no concept of paper money or stamps. All they know is a card slides into plastic machines at checkout stands and purchases are made. So if you grew up with that, how could you possibly understand the concept of your actions online and how it could cost you a job? This is a teaching opportunity for us as parents. There is no way you could understand that concept unless it was taught to you. Older generations grew up understanding that what you 'put in writing' mattered. Years ago we had contracts that had to have a wet signature in order to be valid. Today, documents are put in PDF format and sent from a computer.

While Generation Y may not understand the consequences of social media, they bring a lot of good things to the table. Qualities such as their enthusiasm for work and embracing technology put them ahead of the pack. It is sometimes these same qualities that make older workers feel insecure. Perhaps we should teach them better online behavior and pass on what we've learned.

There is a balance to strike with online profiles and I think it boils down to this: Managers, do not believe everything you read. Some of it is bragging. Job seekers, beware of what you post. Someone is lurking. Please do not let it cost you the job.

I dare you—Google yourself!

Chapter 9
Passing the Phone Interview

The phone interview always feels awkward. Part of it is worrying that you are talking too much or too little. Like uncharted water without a compass, it is difficult to navigate, partially because you cannot see the person's face or get clues from body language. It is a two sided conversation not done in person, with one party asking questions, trying to assess if you are even worth their time to drag you into a face–to-face interview and introduce you to the group.

Expect that phone interviews are a preliminary step to the business relationship. The questions will likely be about basic information with your resume in front of them, asking about your last job, why you left, and your skill set. All employers want to be wanted, so they may want to know why you are interested in their position and how you heard about them. Be complimentary. Companies love when you have taken the time to do the research and know something about them. Bring something of value to the conversation other than just you and your skill set, keeping in mind that you get to ask a few questions as well. Remember, you would be tying up your time in a face-to-face interview too. Make sure it is worth you taking time off from work and getting your suit out of the dry cleaners. And, if it is not a fit, this short conversation allows both parties to recognize that and bow out gracefully.

Phone interviews are meant to glean bits of information quickly without consuming a lot of time. They can be done with Human Resources or with the Hiring Manger, depending on how far along the hiring process is, and also how quick they want to fill the position. You can bet that if Human Resources is conducting the phone screen that is a sign that the conversation will be about twenty to thirty minutes and they will want broad brushstrokes of information. They will judge the promptness of your response and your tone of voice. They will be taking notes. These notes get passed onto the hiring manager with their recommendations to pursue you as a candidate or not. Do not expect the phone screen to be technical in nature, as they will just want to know basic things about you. They will steer away from candidates who lack a clear story and the ability to articulate their work history. Shortly stated, they are looking for flags or clues to NOT hire you, so do not give them any reason.

On the contrary, you would be surprised how many candidates get in front of managers just because they bothered to pop a handwritten thank-you note in the mail to the HR Manager that bothered to conduct the phone screen. Treating HR like glorified administrators that you could care less about will not move you forward on the board, so do not do that, no matter how silly you think their questions are. Many of these HR Managers do not understand what you do. Explain it to them, nicely. No one likes being treated like the village idiot.

Hiring managers conducting the phone screen have the same objective in mind, and it's to save time and get the basics down on paper about you before you meet with them and the team. These phone conversations may go a bit deeper on the technical aspect, but typically will not last more than a half an hour. If you did it right, you get the invitation for a face-to-face interview.

Dead air is a killer in the phone screen. If you find there are long pauses after you spoke, consider they are writing down the information on your resume or on a notebook to capture the necessary part of the conversation for future reference. Silence is okay. It just means they are recording or processing the information you gave them. If this still makes you uncomfortable, it is completely acceptable to ask, "Did I answer your question completely?" They will guide you through and let you know if they want more information or less, and this breaks down the barrier of not being able to see them and judge by their body language if you are going on and on or not.

Common questions you can expect in any phone screen are:

Tell me about your current job and why you are looking.

How did you hear about us?

Tell me about your last job and job history.

Tell me a little bit about the relevant skills you have for this job.

What are your salary expectations?

How soon could you start?

The last two questions do pop up on phone screens because, again, they do not want to take a lot of time getting to know a candidate to then find they are out of the price range and not viable. The employer knows what they can spend and what they cannot. This is also your chance to terminate the interview process if the salary does not match what you need.

Questions around start date are more about giving notice and the employer's urgency to fill the job. This is a dead giveaway that they want it filled and either it has been open for a while, or the workload is becoming unmanageable.

I do recommend that you ask your fair share of questions in the phone interview as well. Process driven questions are best and you will need these to gauge whether it's a job you want or not. Ask your questions toward the end of the conversation. HR Managers are designed to be very helpful and are happy to respond to such questions as:

Although I did read the job description, would you tell me a little bit about the job?

Why is the position open?

How many candidates are you interviewing?

Tell me about the hiring process. Where am I at in that process?

Would you please tell me a little bit about the company culture and values?

When will I hear back?

The last question is critical. There is nothing worse than taking time out of your busy day only to find that you are not what they are looking for in a candidate.

While phone interviews can make you break out into a cold sweat, it does not need to be that way. Go prepared for the meeting, take a deep breath and tell them a little bit about who you are and what makes you a unique candidate.

The objective is always to get invited to the face-to-face interview so you can dazzle them!

Chapter 10
Preparing for Panel Interviews

The most nerve-wracking thing for a candidate is the dreaded panel interview. And frankly, I can think of nothing more unsettling.

Imagine being invited into a conference room with three to five people sitting around you, all asking questions about your work history. It does not foster an atmosphere of acceptance. Surely you feel judged at best, and like a bug under a microscope at worst. Regardless, as I said before, the only way out is through. I guess that is what is so difficult about the job search. You have to apply online, network and find the right opportunity, and it's still not over. You have to get through the interview process itself and hope that you are chosen for the job. It's one hurdle after another.

The reason a panel interview is unsettling for a candidate is the uncertainty of where the power lies in the room. With five people present, and only one asking questions, it leaves you to wonder if the person dominating the room has the ultimate decision to hire and fire you. And if that is so, why not just meet with them individually?

The best way to handle a panel interview is to get as much information as you can about each participant prior to the actual meeting. Typically HR will schedule the interview, and it is appropriate that you ask them for everyone's name and title. Ask also if all parties will be in the room at once, or if you will be meeting with each person individually for the interview, because that does change things a bit. The best scenario is if you can meet with them individually, giving you an opportunity to control the conversation and establish a connection with them personally and professionally. It is difficult to do that with five people in the same room, and one or two firing questions at you.

Preparation is the key to any panel interview. After you get the manager's names, take some time and do some research on each person that will interview you, trying to understand their role in the company and also their power position. Do not assume the title tells you the power. Organization charts usually dictate the power in a company, although you will certainly figure out who is who once you get into the room. Generally, there will be one person who will lead and dominate the atmosphere. Again, this does not necessary mean that they hold the total decision making power, but it would be wise to take note of that. Minimally, it tells you that they need a high sense of control, which gives you insight to how they will act if they worked with you on a daily basis.

When conducting the research, look on LinkedIn and also Google. Get a general sense for each person in terms of where they went to college, what area of the country they grew up in, what jobs they have held in the past and how long they have been with the company in this position. Online profiles paint a picture of who they are, and, if you look closely, can give you a deeper insight into their values. One's geographical place of origin will tell you a lot about a person. Where they went to school and how long they held their last job will also tell you something about what they value. Read, notice patterns and keep this information in the back of your mind.

For example, I did this exact exercise with a Project Manager who was a client of mine. He got invited to an interview and was not confident about how to proceed. The first thing we did was take the recruiter's name and went onto LinkedIn. We discovered that she had been with her firm about three years, but had been a recruiter in an agency setting for nearly eight years. That told us that she was seasoned enough to be trusted with his career and to be able to give him guidance. Working in an agency is much grittier than working as a recruiter internally. She would have to have guts and drive to succeed. If not for that background, she would likely be working an HR job with a short stint in an agency, which would lead me to believe that she was better at process and less skilled at selling. Like it or not, headhunting is not really about being friendly and finding you a job. It is a hardcore sales position that says if you make your billings you get to stay. If you do not, you are fired. Clearly, this young woman knew what she was doing or she would not have been there for eight years in the field. We also noted the amount of groups that she was connected to, which told us she was well networked in the business community, and did work after hours, attending social functions to continue to build her business. A networked recruiter is worth their weight in gold and will pay dividends. We also saw that she graduated with a degree in communications. Here is a person you can trust!

Next, we looked up the name of the manager who would be a part of the interview process. It turned out he was an engineering manager with a Bachelors of Science who had focused early as an electrical engineer early in his career. Good tie-in with my client, since he studied the same field twenty years ago. At least they would have something to talk about. Also, as a leader, this manager would know immediately if the work was done correctly or not because he had obviously held that job earlier in his career. There is nothing worse than reporting to someone who does not know a thing about what you do at your desk. Digging further, we discovered that the manager had held three other positions in high tech companies, telling me that he preferred the fast moving environment. He had also worked his way up in each position before he left. This is all good information and worth knowing before you walk into the conference room for the interview.

Gathering this type of data allows a person to eliminate any surprises in the interview process. Believe me, they have already looked you up online to review your background, as well as read your resume. Fair is fair. If they can gather information about you, you can certainly gather information about them prior to the interview. Again, you are not making a judgment call, but trying to better understand who they are before you walk into a panel interview.

The rule of thumb is if the interview is conducted by Human Resources, their line of questioning will be around company culture and fit. The interview will be more general and you can elaborate as much as you want. Their final say may or may not hold any weight in the hiring decision. That depends on how well they are respected in the company. Some organizations just use Human Resources as a preliminary screening process, then expect the hiring manager to dig deeper in the interview. Other Human Resource professionals will have a background in Organizational Development. Never misjudge and confuse them with a typical HR admin function. Do not let them fool you, for they are not company party planners. Other HR Managers have a dual function between accounting and HR. Recruiting is not their primary function, and obviously, they will not have a large say in the hiring decision.

Regardless of how intense and respected the HR person's role is, you have to get through them in order to graduate to the next step. Answer their questions honestly and directly. They are the main key to you getting inside.

The only thing that may creep up unexpectedly is behavioral interview questions. There is no amount of preparation for these, so it is best to just answer honestly. Consider all of this if they pop up as part of the panel interview team.

Behavioral interview questions always start with a tone for the worst, pointing toward your history in an assumptive fashion and then determining by your response how you will act in the future. These questions will always start with, "Tell me about a time when..." That's your flag that you're rolling into the behavioral interview question and there is no dodging. Just answer as best you can and move on.

In a panel interview, eye contact and building rapport with each person in the room is critical. You want to make sure that you answered each person's question directly, and given him or her all the information they need. If one person dominated the interview, try to speak to the entire group.

Although panel interviews are nerve wracking, a good strategy when answering panel questions is to cross reference a question with one that has already been asked by a different member. For example, *"To expand on my answer to John, my experience in product management also includes..."* This reinforces your original statements already discussed and addresses the concerns of two panel members at once. Do not be alarmed if the panel members take notes during your interview answer. Use it as a reminder that you need to speak clearly and concisely. Panel interviews are designed because it's a way to get all the hiring managers in the room together and judge by consensus. They are also conducted in the interest of time, although they are not always effective. The result is now there are too many people involved in the hiring decision.

Taking notes is a sign that you listen and are reflective. I recommended that as you sit down, you ask permission to take notes. I have never heard of a case where the interviewers declined the request. Taking notes gives the perception that you are engaged and care enough about the process to jot down important details. The notebook should also contain your questions for them at the end.

Remember, each person in the panel interview will come from their unique perspective and will be thinking about how your job would impact theirs if you were to be hired. For example, the technical manager will dig deeply into your technical skills. They may ask questions that are not even relevant to the job at hand, so if you find the conversation going off into an unfamiliar area, stop them and ask them, "Why is that? It sounds as if that skill is important. How does it tie into the project?" Minimally, this will snap them into the present moment; making them realize that it perhaps is of no bearing after all. It also protects your perception. The last thing you want is a big red stamp of 'NOT QUALIFIED" on your file because the conversation took a tangent immaterial to the job at hand. Panel interviews have a way of derailing and getting off track due to the open forum.

If you do not have all the skill experience needed for the job, it's okay. Don't panic. Employers want to get the most skill they can for the dollar they pay you. Answer honestly, with your willingness to learn the skill, and then reemphasize where you are qualified. No candidate is perfect.

For some interviews, a CFO will be present in the panel interview. Same thought process. All you need to know is accountants are numbers people and will want to know data and numbers around who you are, and your deliverables. They are fact-finding types of people. Talk to them in facts and numbers. Their thought process will be linear without pitfalls and potholes. Trust that what they are asking is important and respond accordingly.

Sales people or marketing people taking part in the panel interview will typically be warm and friendly. However, beware of the exterior, as they will have a motive for getting you into the job or keeping you out due to competition. That will all depend on how secure they are within themselves and within their jobs. Their line of questioning could be all over the board, making it difficult to predict.

A graceful closing to the panel interview is like a cherry on top of a cupcake. Shake each person's hand and thank them for their time, making sure that you get a business card from each of them. After the interview, on the same day, handwrite a thank you card to each of them and mail it. This keeps your candidacy on the top of their mind long after you left the conference room. The note should be fairly short and professional. Do NOT ask for the job, or re-emphasize why you would be good there or how much you would like to work with them. It's a thank you note, not a sales tactic. The purpose of the note is to thank them for their time and to express gratitude, and it could be a place to compliment them on their organization, but that is it. The thank you note will actually set you apart from other candidates who did not write one at all or just shot a simple 'Thank you' email with those words in the subject line.

These are just behind-the-scenes tricks that I learned from interviewing thousands of hiring managers and getting feedback from thousands of candidates. It works. Try not to over think it. Do the research, look at the data and make basic conclusions about who they are before you go to the interview.

Panel interviews need not fill you with terror, because this time you will know what to expect.

Take a deep breath, lean back, relax and tell us about yourself.

Chapter 11
Manage Your References

At last! You have gotten through the interview and they are about to extend an offer, but first they want to check a few references. Are you ready?

Managing your references is the critical piece everyone forgets to do. We all get so caught up in the job process, concerned about applying online perfectly, getting the interview, getting *through* the interview—that we do not pay much attention to our references. We consider the deal is nearly done, but in fact the references can make or break employment. Some candidates naively think these calls will not even be made.

I have personally conducted reference checks for years, and although they are scripted, it is amazing what managers will tell you if you just ask. I know that there is this whole idea that a manager cannot verify anything but names and dates or they will get sued, but do not count on that after you leave. Choose your references carefully. Know that they have your best interest in mind after you leave.

Without careful preparation your reference check can be a disaster waiting to happen. For example, during my career as a headhunter, I once had the dicey experience of conducting reference checks and disclosing them all to my client, never realizing that he double-checked and called each of the references himself. I was never sure what prompted him to do that, but he came across a bit of information that would forever change the candidate's ability to get hired. Through his calls, he realized that the candidate had worked for a competitor, and my client had friends there. What was initially a reference check turned into a gossip session when my client was informed that the candidate, a female engineer, had a sordid affair with her married male boss. The engineering team members she worked with at the time knew about the affair and suspected that she got special treatment. When the recession hit, the man with whom she had an affair eliminated her position, wanting to remove her from the organization and avoid rumors that would hurt his position as a manager. Not knowing any of this, she came to me as a candidate looking for work. Throughout my interview process and checking, she looked fine. Assessing her as an excellent candidate, I was very excited to work with her, knowing I could place her immediately. I did my diligence. I interviewed her, called her references, and at the last minute, my client rejected her. Once I found out why, I was unsure of how to handle the delicate situation. By law, I could not disclose what was uncovered, nor did I intend on having that conversation with my candidate. But, obviously we could not staff her, either. The story ended with the candidate being rejected by the manager, me telling her she was not a good fit for the position and that was it.

In the recruiting business we call these reference checks 'off the cuff'. It means that you call the listed references, but if you can, you call others you know from other companies, asking about the character of the candidate. This happens in the accounting profession all the time. A Manager or Partner of a CPA firm will call the Partner of another CPA firm to find out if they know anything about the candidate. If your work is not good, or you have no intention of getting your CPA and moving up the chain, it comes out over the telephone wire. All you know is you did not get the job.

I have also seen the flip side in which a reference did tip the scales between two close candidates for the same job. The stronger reference wins. Employers look for references to be balanced, fair and at the very best, glowing. A glowing reference is one where you can hear the enthusiasm for the candidate in the reference's voice.

All is fair in love, war and business.

And while this all seems unfair and daunting, it is best to control what you can in the process. It is a shame to have the reference be the make or break of you getting the position.

References have a way of uncovering your behavior in the workplace, and not just your skill. While these are fair questions, it is also loaded—from your perspective. Think of it from the employer's side. This is about more than just your skills and can you do the job. It is about playing in the playground and getting along. Co-workers who dislike working with you will affect the team and, ultimately, production. Generally speaking, people only buy what solves their problem and what makes them feel good. In terms of the job search, if the employer likes you and finds you competent, you get the job. It's that simple. Now add a strong reference to the list of what they think you do right, and you just landed yourself a new job. Product sold. And that product, like it or not, is you!

Managing your references is a three-step process:
1st Gain permission to use your reference
2nd Talk through how they will respond if asked your weaknesses and strengths
3rd Give your reference a heads-up when an employer may be calling

It is amazing how many times I have called a reference only to find the manager not willing to speak to me, or not bothering to call me back. That is a red flag that says the candidate isn't all that hot. Remember, your reference should be your cheerleader and tip the scales, making the employer feel excited about hiring you. By the time the person checking the references hangs up the phone, they should feel confident that they are getting the best employee available. A reference should be credible, honest and frank about discussing your strengths and limitations. Choose your references carefully. Make sure they will represent you fairly and, most importantly, make sure that they *want* to do this for you. References should be from people you reported to, and not co-workers or direct reports. When listing the reference, get permission to use their work phone or their cell phone. List their name, title, email address and company name. Keep the information current. If you both worked at a previous company, use their current workplace when you list them on your reference sheet, but explain in parenthesis where you had worked together and what the reporting relationship was.

For example:
John Terrance, Vice President
212-891-1257 work
212-467-9009 cell
Wells Fargo Bank
(Formerly VP at Key Bank)
I reported to John at Key Bank.

Talk with your references about how they would describe your strengths. This is always surprising to most candidates. What you think your strength was in the workplace may not match their idea. Heck, they may have a better response. Perhaps they are missing where you really stepped up on a project because they were too busy doing their job. Either way, it helps to understand their perspective. And, always ask how they would respond to answering questions around your limitations. Again, you want this to be an honest response, but you also do not want them going down certain paths. Remember, limitations are your strengths blown out of proportion under stress.

Here is an illustration of a comment given during a reference check showing a balanced response that helped the candidate land the job. "Under stress, Jamie can be viewed as controlling, which is also her best strength. I knew if I handed her a project it would get done."

"Mike's limitation is his tendency to overwork. After so many hours, it's impossible to be effective. Ensure he goes home and gets some rest so he can perform for you the next day."

"Lisa is better at seeing the big picture and sometimes misses details. However, because she is so goal orientated, she is highly effective and always delivers great results."

These candid responses tell the potential employer about you while not overselling. We all know that an employee has a limitation or weakness, and believe it or not, employers are willing to sign up for that. The reference just tells us what to expect and will give additional information to a leader.

The job hunt could take you months, so keep your references updated. Statistically, the entire hiring process with any company from the moment they post the ad until they go to offer spans six to eight weeks. Meaning: the references you collected and gave three months ago forgot you were on the job hunt. Stay in touch with them. It's polite. They are doing a favor for you, and you should check in every few weeks or so to say hello and let them know you are looking.

The most powerful way to leverage a reference, in a case where you feel you are close to being offered the job, is to give your reference a heads up and a copy of the job description so they can tailor their comments specifically to the job you are applying for. This way when they get the call from the potential employer, they can speak directly to that open position and how you are best suited for that job.

Managing references is that small detail that no one really thinks about, but it can be your biggest asset. And like a gift well received, remember to give this same courtesy back when you are a reference for someone else during his/her job hunt.

Chapter 12
Counter Offer Conundrum

Looking for a job while you have a job feels so sneaky. Let's be honest; it also feels very satisfying! There you are, in your cube or office, looking at postings on Craigslist or Indeed.com, dreaming of greener pastures. There is a secretive feeling of the satisfaction of the final exit. Righteousness floods your veins as you imagine the pleasure of giving notice and walking away from an employer. Not unlike leaving an unfaithful lover, leaving an employer who mistreated you can ignite the irresistible sensation of revenge. The 'You'll miss me when I'm gone' syndrome. These feelings are not just reserved for jilted lovers and bitter single moms, but also for the unappreciated workers who have endured long terms of service and are tired of taking it!

I think we've all been there.

You're wishing and hoping that the employer will be devastated when you give notice, and pack your belongings in a cardboard box, and head through the lobby to your car for the last time. You anticipate the relief that will sweep over, a relief that that says you are finally free! Free of the stress and tension just knowing you will never have to see them again.

Just don't be surprised if your parting conversation does not turn out as planned. It may not. In fact, I would expect and prepare for a counter offer as the job market gets tighter and good people become harder to find. Does that surprise you? They might let you go without a fight, but always be prepared for a counter offer.

Here is how it plays out when it all goes sideways.

Mike had planned this moment for months, and finally landed an excellent job with a transportation company in another city. The offer was fair and it was a step up for him in his career path. He had met his new boss and coworkers and was ready to give his two weeks notice at nine am on a Monday morning. It just did not go as smoothly as he had hoped. He had neglected to write a letter of resignation, hoping instead to just have a quick ten-minute conversation with his boss and leave it at that. Although he was a bit nervous approaching his boss that morning, a smug feeling came over him. This was the day he finally got to tell them to stick it.

"John? Do you have a few moments? I need to talk with you." Mike stood in the doorway of the cool office.

Looking over his spreadsheets, John pushed aside his paperwork as Mike sat down.

"John, I've accepted another position as a General Manager. I'm here to give my notice."

Stunned and clearly caught off guard, John looked at Mike in a calculating manner. He tried not to show the shock on his face, but was doing a poor job. Yes, he knew he had been overworking Mike for months, and he did have to deny him his vacation time last month.

The business had been hit hard for the past two years with customers downsizing and cutting their orders. The company had also lost its biggest account, reducing its yearly revenue by about ten million. John himself had been working close to sixty hours a week for the past nine months. Tired, he failed to see that he was losing Mike, having ignored many warning signs that may have been there. Frankly, he had been too busy trying to save the little business they had. He had been working with less staff due to the reductions in force they took two years ago, just to stay afloat. He was not ready for this conversation. He was not ready at all. Mike was one of his best employees and had given the company ten years of service. There was no reason to anticipate his leaving the company now.

"Where are you going?" John asked carefully.

"I took another position at American Roadways. I start on the fifteenth." This was Mike's first mistake of many in giving his notice. Employers can ask where you are going, but it is not always wise to tell them.

"Did they give you more money? Is that what this is about?" John drilled down.

"Yes, they gave me about ten thousand more a year and a company car. The benefit package is good, too. I can finally cover my kids at no cost on the healthcare," Mike stated, sharing too much.

"Mike, we can match that. If you wanted more money, you should have just said so. You are an important team member. I can't do anything about our benefit plan, but I can certainly give you an extra 10 thousand a year. In fact, just to show you what you mean to the company, I'll give you twelve thousand more a year. How is that?"

Mike was stunned. Here was his boss offering him more money and more attentiveness than he had been given in months. You practically had to make an appointment a week in advance to talk to this guy, and now suddenly he had his attention.

"Well, I don't know. I'm supposed to start in a couple of weeks." Mike hesitated. He realized that he could stay where he was and not make any changes at all. He had given them ten years of service. Although his current job was not perfect, starting a new position was scary and he knew it. Heck, he could come in with a roaring case of the flu and do the current job with his eyes closed if needed. The other piece was he knew everyone. He had seen employees come and go, but he was a part of the core group, and had felt that way until two years ago.

"Think it over. Let me know this afternoon. I'll put in the paperwork to HR for the pay grade increase. And, you know...you really should take that time off. I'm sorry you had to cancel that trip to Disney Land with your kids last month. It was just so busy here and we really needed you." John responded. His desperate attempt to connect was obvious.

Mike left the office confused, wondering what to do.

Never let this happen to you. Expect a counter offer. Draft a short and direct letter of resignation prior to your meeting. Email it the night before you walk in and give the verbal notice the following morning. This gives your employer a heads up and also shows a written record that will be forwarded to HR.

A resignation letter should read like this:

Dear John,

As of yesterday I have accepted another position and will be leaving this organization. After long and careful consideration, my decision is final.

I'm thankful for the opportunity and career growth I have been afforded over the years, and will help you and the staff through my transition.

My final day of work will be April 15.

Best Regards,

Mike Collins

Look at that letter carefully. It immediately dismisses any chance of counter offer by stating your decision is final and that you have thought long and hard about it. Sending the letter the evening prior gives them time to digest it; and think about your replacement and necessary steps to transition you out of the system. It is a fair, decent and professional approach.

Terminating any relationship is difficult if you allow emotions to get in the way. Don't allow ego driven fantasies to cloud your judgment. Set the stage and control the conversation all the way out the door.

When Ellie left her job after twenty-five years of service, she had butterflies in her stomach. The decision to leave came naturally, and a month prior the organization had warned her that her job might be ending in six months. No job magically ends after twenty-five years, and Ellie knew that as well as I did. This was a political scene playing out that had nothing to do with her performance. It was time for her to muster up some courage and find a new place to work. She did, but the actually announcing to her boss that she was leaving made her uncomfortable—and nauseous.

To her surprise, the notice of her leaving sent a loud ripple through the organization, and each day she was fielding phone calls asking her if she was being forced to quit. I urged her not to give information to others because doing so would only fuel the rumors. Ellie gave short responses about her leaving her job, but gave no details about where she was going or why. I coached her to answer a question with a question and ask them in return how she could best help them through the transition of her departure. Eventually, with her response, the questions died down and Ellie was able to control the perception right out the door.

People around you will become fearful when they see you leaving. They will wonder if you got a better deal in terms of pay, and if their job is safe. All sorts of odd things come into people's minds when someone leaves, especially if the person worked for the company for a long time. Remember however, that it is not your job to ensure their comfort. It is your job to manage the transition and be respectful to your employer.

It's fair. They gave you a place to work and to apply your creative force for money in return. You took their money and gave your time. And that is where it ends. It's a business relationship, not a family; do not confuse the two. These people called coworkers are not really your 'friends' either; because when push comes to shove and it's their job or yours, guess what they choose? Chances are, after you leave and have your goodbye party and cake in the conference room, you will not talk to them again.

All relationships end eventually, and they should. It means you have grown and changed. It means you are unwilling to accept less than what you deserve. It is also a statement that if your needs are not met, you will go get them met elsewhere. There is nothing wrong with that. People leave jobs for different reasons. Perhaps you leave because you want to expand your skills and learn more and you cannot do it there anymore. You feel topped out and stagnant working there. Like a marriage that has been over for years and yet you continue to stay, a job can become a distorted type of relationship where a person can confuse loyalty and guilt. After the fear dissolves and you are ready to move on, they cannot hold you captive any longer. However, your responsibility to them is not terminated until you actually leave. Do the right thing and walk them through the process gently. Keep your mind on your transition, not on what awaits you beyond the door.

I have also seen departures go so smoothly that the employer felt thankful to the employee that was leaving. Brian, a senior project engineer, departed from his last job at a high tech company with class. He had given them seven years of service, straightened out numerous processes and always responded patiently when the organization resisted change. He had a way of selling his ideas and gracefully waiting until they could integrate the change. Anyone working there could point to his obvious contributions to the company, his boss included. Regardless, one day it was no longer working for him and he asked me to find him another position. Within three months he had a position with a twenty thousand dollar increase and a huge title promotion, which was too good to refuse. We talked through how to break the news of his new job to the boss and the company to which he had been devoted for so many years. Showing his excitement would be distasteful, so I cautioned him to choose his words carefully. Together, we wrote his letter of resignation and I coached him through the conversation. The next morning came together beautifully, and Brian ended up leaving with his laptop as a parting gift and several weeks of extra project work at high pay as a contractor, which was work he could do on his off time. The company really valued him, and seeing a departure unfold like this was a first for me. Brian got to walk off into the sunset to a better job; and secure another five thousand dollars of side work, a pay increase and his old laptop.

Counter offers are always a slippery slope and it is best to be prepared in case the conversation takes place.

What is best for you in the long run is to leave your employer with their dignity.

Always leave a job with grace. Your departure shouldn't harm others in the process.

Chapter 13
Show Me The Money!

Let me start this chapter by stating that money itself has no power.

For years I have been asked questions about how to negotiate salaries, with good reason. People considered me the expert, and I guess I earned that recognition. Even my own family seems to see me as the magician when it comes to money. I'm not so sure about that. I know how to ask for it and I know how to spend it. To me it's simple addition and subtraction. And it's as simple as you have it, or you don't. If you don't have it, don't spend ahead. I live my life by this principal.

Money is not emotional and cannot make you feel bad or sad. It has no power over you at all. The only power it has is that which you attach to it. Your belief about money originally came from somewhere else, either from your parents or grandparents, and as adults I suggest people examine their beliefs from time to time. They are not always truths. They are things people told you that you latched onto. The issue with beliefs around money is that they will hinder your career decisions and cripple you in terms of what you could be making. Many a person with low self-esteem is poor. Likewise, many egomaniacs look like they have a lot but can't pay a parking meter downtown.

I always found it amusing that for a living I negotiated people's salaries, and I found myself thankful for my beliefs around money. For ten years as a headhunter, candidates depended on me to negotiate the wages of their next job, banking on me (no pun intended) to get them more income. Rightfully so, I never broke into a sweat when talking about money. Money means nothing to me. Well, I guess that's not true. When I buy gas for the car or a new pair of shoes, then it does hold some value to me. But overall, I guess I'm saying that it doesn't scare me.

Greenbacks produce neither fear, nor a sense of lack in me.

Part of it is my internal belief that there is *enough*. There is enough money, enough time and enough for me to get some in my pocket. I never worry about that. I have always been able to create money even out of the hardest times. I have always had more than enough and I credit my impartial, non-emotional view of money as the thing that has enabled me to find jobs for hundreds of candidates. It's my belief that there is enough, and that they can have more, which allows me to seal the deal.

Money is nothing but energy in motion.

It is meant to come into your wallet and go back out.

In fact, our fine country was founded on that concept. Just look at what happens to the stock market and the economy when we clamp down and tighten up in fear. Everything stops. Money is meant to be mobile. It's meant to be earned, spent, and saved. So why do we get anxious when we talk about *our* money?

If American dollars were puga shells would it seem different to you? If you went into the store and exchanged twenty puga shells for three bags of groceries and a bottle of water, would the exercise be different? What if it were not puga shells, but rocks? Would that change your idea about money?

Not really.

In Western society we are taught to chase money at an early age. The haves and the have-nots surround us. We vainly believe having more is better, and that having more will equate to happiness.

Chasing money never got anyone anyplace but exhausted.

However, there is a huge difference between concern over money and outright fear of money.

Think back to the puga shell concept of money exchange. Did you see what I did? I reduced money to the ridiculous so you could see it differently. I took the emotion (not the truth) out of the *concept* of money in order to shift your reality.

Most of us grew up with beliefs about money that we held onto long into our adulthood, and that do not serve us any longer. Furthermore, these views tend to hold us hostage to our own financial ruin. For example, were you told growing up that 'money doesn't grow on trees'? Did you hear your parents fight over money? Did you ever fear you would end up being the bag lady or can man on the street? It amazes me how many six-figure earners I know who fear being homeless. Projecting that fear onto our children will produce adults with real money troubles.

I should re-phrase that. Money is not trouble. YOU have trouble with money (if you allow it), but money itself is not a problem.

Money is a piece of paper. It has no power but what you give it through your views and emotions. As a child, you bought into what you were taught and at any time you can change those thoughts. You believed what they told you, and then built your life around those ideas.

Fact: Those ideas about money were someone else's.

They were not yours.

You came into the world without a view about money, spending, or a vision of how much you would make or what kind of car you would drive.

You slowly made those opinions and formed them into hard beliefs somewhere around the age of eighteen. Oh, you may have gathered data and experiences from age three onward, but you started to filter the data into experience and learning as soon as you got your first job.

And then we all scratch our heads and wonder why we cannot ask for a well-earned raise after five years of hard work.

We wonder why when it comes to the actual discussion about the job offer and compensation you have butterflies in your stomach.

Not surprising, as a matter of fact. No mystery there.

While I cannot undo the wiring in your head that got you this far into adulthood, I can give you some tools and illustrations of how to view money and some language around the conversation about money itself. Money is created; it is not the product of a whim or a chance or even, dare I say, earned. It is created. There is enough money printed and circulating 'out there'. The trick is to get more of it into your wallet. For whatever reason, women have a harder time asking for money than men do. And it also depends on the party with which you are negotiating your salary. For example, if it is two men talking about money and salary, it can get sticky. Men and money can quickly equate to an ego battle instead of a negotiation, so beware. However, if you are talking about salary with a female HR Manager you can expect the conversation to be more collaborative and less combative. Think about who your audience is and what you are worth *before* you get into money conversations. The company's objective is to get the best skill set for the most reasonable price.

Did you know that when a company pays you a salary, there is actually another fifteen percent that goes on top of your wage to cover payroll taxes and benefits? For example, if you make fifty thousand dollars a year, in actuality; the company is paying out of pocket at least sixty-five thousand or more, depending on the benefits offered and the tax structure.

Your objective is to make a progression on your salary and move upward. Always be moving upward in money and try not to make lateral moves if possible. At mid career, you are *expected* to make more and ask for more as you are building your skills and financial wealth. At the sunset of your career, you should be topped out for the skill set, and naturally, other things will be more important to you, such as a company's solvency and the person you report to, rather than making the next ten thousand. And, if you are starting out, well…just get a job. It will all come into focus after you just get a job and keep it for a while. Soft skill sets, good working habits, learning how to work with others and completing a task are the critical building blocks formed in the first job. Just get one. This is not the time to be picky.

Benefits mean money in your pocket, so don't breeze over that section in the offer letter. Look closely at the payouts for medical coverage. How much comes out of your pocket? How much are the co-pays? Does it cover alternative care? Does that matter to you? A good package should cover going to the doctor for a cold or for heart surgery, so beware of the fine print. Know that if there is no coverage, and you need it, you may have to pay for it. Look at dental plans and vision plans carefully. These can be hidden costs that whittle away at your salary, so make sure that you earn enough. One company I knew had a benefit plan that cost employees seven hundred dollars a month out of pocket. The wages they offered were not exactly generous to offset the costs. Dependents cost even more to add on, and the reason the benefit plan was not competitive was because the owner did not want to pay for the cost of the insurance, and because his company was not large enough to offer a competitive plan.

Take advantage of flex spending plans if at all possible. These tax-free dollars add up, and it will surprise you how much difference they make over a year. Just your prescriptions alone add up in a year's time, and that's not counting the unexpected visit to the doctor. The flex spending plan is a way to have that money allocated and put aside, like a rainy day fund. I know every time I go to the doctor's I pay about a hundred bucks. The flex spending allows me to not worry about the added expense that would throw my budget out of whack. These are all things to consider when looking at the offer letter and talking about money. You have to understand exactly how much money you are actually talking about, and have firm numbers. Life is hard to plan without firm numbers.

I think the best way to keep money a neutral thought is by keeping it about numbers and not the value of who you are. *Your salary is not the value of who you are.* It is the value of your skill set, and you get to control that. Go back to school, take a class, finish a degree and you are expected to make more money, within reason, the reason being the market and what the skills command. Any title, any position always commands X number of dollars, which is why postings will sometimes read DOE, or depending on experience. That wording does not mean if they like you they give you a few more bucks. It means they take into consideration how many years of experience you have, any extra credentials, and your overall history and career path within the industries you worked for. All of this equates to your market worth.

How much are you worth? Could you ask for a raise or should you bail out and look for another job entirely? Conduct research before you apply to jobs so you know what the market will bear for the position. Look at job postings to get a sense of salaries and also look at Salary.com, and other sites such as payscale.com, to see what positions pay. Even Indeed.com has a salary section you could view to get some sense of the pay grade for your level of experience. What you get paid now is a benchmark to what you may or may not get paid in the future, and this is good to know long before you start sending out resumes.

During the job search, the first point of contact will be a phone screen. It is not uncommon that the phone interviewer will discuss salary. They do this because: 1) They are unsure what they should be paying and want a baseline, and 2) They want to know if they can afford you if they want to 'buy' you. However, be careful with throwing out the first number.

Think of it as a game of poker, and you play your cards close to the deck. Answer the question with a question and ask the interviewer, "What is the range of the position?" They know what the range is and it should be about a ten thousand dollar spread between the high end and low end of the pay. The hidden mystery is always are they willing and prepared to come to the high end of the range? You would be surprised how many companies have no intention of paying the top end of the scale. I never understood why they put that number out on the table. It is deceiving. They have champagne taste on a beer budget. And, over the years, I have had to have this eye opening conversation with numerous clients. They cannot expect to get all sorts of skill sets with a laundry list of duties and pay next to nothing. They cannot expect to make a hybrid position of administration and accounting and find someone. The job market does not work like that. School and degrees are not attained like that either. Beware of employers with unreasonable expectations. While it is good to be needed, you do not want to become a Jack or Jill of all trades with a diluted skill set.

I will warn you that if you've survived recession, and now find yourself doing the jobs of three people, it is possible that you do so much your skill set is diluted. You may be underpaid. You may not even have a job title that matches your duties anymore. This just happens as a cause and effect of the survivors of recession. The company laid people off, kept you, and now here you are. Take that into consideration if you do decide to ask for a raise. Outline what you did before, and what you do now. If they are vastly different, ask for role clarity and more money, if appropriate. You may decide it's time to leave the company altogether. Conversations about money should be unemotional and professional.

Another helpful tool to use during negotiations is to pretend that you are talking about someone else's money, and not yours. You may be more inclined to stand up and get what you deserve if you think of it from a third-person perspective.

To illustrate, here is an example of how to negotiate a higher salary.

Manager: "Bill, I see that you've made eighty thousand in the past. What are your expectations for this marketing position?"

You: "Well, considering the skill level that you need, coupled with the responsibility of the job, I think that between eighty-five and ninety thousand would be fair."

If that number surprises them or they begin to object, have three solid reasons why you deserve the money. Do not blink. _Silence does not mean no. It means they are thinking about it._

Manager: Well, I don't know. That's a little higher than we wanted to pay.

You: I am confident that within the first quarter, with some understanding of how your operation works, I can reduce headcount while getting the team to perform at a higher level. I will do this by assessing the current staff, making adjustments if need be, and putting in a metrics system that tracks production. Let me remind you that in my last position, I pioneered a new channel, got my staff performing at a higher level with less people on the team, all within two years. I hired, trained and developed all of my staff and went out on sales calls when necessary. The system I can implement is solid. So, I think eighty-five and ninety thousand is fair considering the needs of your organization.

People are reasonable for the most part. Showing them what you have of value and equating that to money seals the deal. I have used the above concept and it has worked in candidate negotiations, as well as when bidding for projects on my own. Money is never an emotional issue or something I shy away from talking about. I have a firm understanding that it is what makes the world go 'round.

Sadly, sometimes, you don't get the salary you requested. When that happens, you have to be strong enough to say no if the pay is too low. It is okay to say no. Accepting low pay tells yourself that you have low worth. Over time, accepting low pay becomes a hard habit to break.

For example, Julie called me one morning and told me about an offer she had received after nine months of unemployment in a region of the country where it seemed impossible to find work.

I could hear the conflict in her voice as she described the interview process and what was said, "Elizabeth, it's going to be a lot of hours. And for the money, at fifty-eight years old, I'm just not sure I want all that overtime. It's not that I'm lazy or won't work hard. It's just they are all so dedicated and live and die for the company. I'm afraid to reject the offer and I'm afraid to get hired." We talked through this quite a bit and I gave her permission to say no, considering the pay, the hours and where she was in her stage of life. As fate would have it, she was not offered the job. The exercise itself allowed her the possibility of saying no, and rejecting them changed her for life. It gave her the confidence to trust herself and stand by what she really wanted.

Money, jobs, savings, life and retirement will always be at the forefront of our minds, and all of these things should be, to some extent. The idea is to balance the job, money and your life to complete *your* picture. Creating a map of what your life should look like is important, as opposed to getting thrown from job to job and place to place.

Simply: Don't ask, don't get!

PART TWO
THEM (The Employer)

Chapter 14
What a Boss Really Looks for in You

We have just completed the first section of the book, which talks about you as the prospective candidate and job seeker. The second section is about the employer and will help you to understand what is on their agenda during the hiring process. Consider this section the little black book of manager's secrets revealed, so that you can best understand and position yourself.

As an illustration, I'd like to tell you about my latest client. John was one of the brightest individuals that I've worked with over the years, mostly because he had the courage to ask "why" in our sessions. I mentioned to him that most engineers ask "how", and not "why", and that was the difference in a brilliant mind. During one of our meetings he asked sincerely, "Why do employers hire this way, Elizabeth? Is there a process that they follow to get a good candidate?" The "why" question forces you to dig deeper and look beneath the surface. He made it clear that he did not understand how an employer thought, and John's conundrum was the inspiration for this chapter.

John explained that if I could give readers the other side of the equation we would all do a better at the job search, and I agreed. While I can give dozens of "how to" examples that work, there is nothing quite like cracking open someone's brain (like the manager's) and seeing how it ticks. Most jobseekers find the process of job searching frustrating because it does not entirely make sense to them. Applying online, interviewing, and the overall process has an element of mystery to it. This chapter will shed some light.

John's first and biggest mistake was the assumption of a *job process* from the employer's perspective. He thought that job descriptions were talked about and written by hiring managers that came to a consensus on the project at hand before a job was posted. Furthermore, he thought that when you applied, the person on the other side of the desk would be able to draw conclusions from your resume regarding what you did. He thought, looking at his own resume, certainly the reader would understand that he could in fact do the job posted. In actuality, John gave HR, or whoever was the first pass at his resume, too much credit.

Unfortunately, it *never* works that way. There is no job process in most companies. Old job descriptions are posted, someone reviews resumes and they may or may not get to the hiring manager. I'm sorry to have to break it to you, but most of the job search is a crapshoot.

Unsettling as it may be to read, it's true. Knowing this makes a job-seeker feel as if they will never get through to the other side of the maze and into the organization.

Understand that there is a margin of error between the actual job posting and the job itself. Most companies have a job description, but do not know what skills they really want in a candidate until they read a pile of resumes. That exercise usually tells them what they don't want, but few organizations actually re-write the ad and post it again.

From your perspective as the jobseeker, the margin of error is as big or as small as your interview. You control the interview process by asking questions. If you fail to ask the right questions to uncover what the job really is, the margin of error goes up. Keep in mind, the margin of error will determine your level of happiness in your new position, so it is in your best interest to ask questions and really understand what the company needs and wants. You can never remove the margin of error, but you can lessen your chances of getting another job that doesn't fit. The only way to lessen the margin of error is to ask specific questions about the leadership, the job itself, and the company as a whole. Oddly enough, many managers do not even know what they want, in terms of qualities and skills, until you walk in the door. They treat the hiring process as glorified window shopping, hoping the right candidate will reveal themselves to them and a big A-HA! moment will occur. While it may be poor planning, I was never surprised to learn that many managers viewed interviewing this way. They told me they were too busy and preferred to go into interviews flying by the seat of their pants. There was no check sheet, no process, and no recipe that made a good employee for them. The lack of planning also gave them a mishmash of skills and personalities in the department. While not all organizations are run in this manner, some are, and you should be wary of that.

Let's start from the beginning. By the time you see a position posted, one of three things has already happened; someone quit, someone was fired or someone went on maternity leave and did not come back. It's that simple.

Employers post the ad under pressure, typically two weeks too late, desperate to replace the former employee so that they can get back to business. As absurd as it sounds, most job descriptions are written five years before they reach your eyes, and posted without the current manager's approval. Old salaries, old job duties and old qualifications are listed. These jobs are posted without thought or review. The lesson for you is don't live and die by the posted job descriptions. I have seen job seekers ignore a posting because it did not seem interesting or exciting, which is foolish. Until you meet the employer, it is impossible to ascertain the nature of the job or the kinds of people you would be working with. Furthermore, employers are not sure exactly what the job needs to entail or who the 'perfect person' is until they meet candidates in person. They do have some idea of the actual skills needed, but that's about it. If it feels like a fishing exposition, you are right on some level. Employers like to try out people in the interview process and then tighten up the job description. However, in a tight job market where there are more job openings than people, this tactic backfires quickly.

Old postings and open jobs should cause concern for you as you flip through the ads online. Seeing the same job posted over and over again for months is a red flag. This means the employer is having a difficult time deciding who is right for the job, and has decided to go through every candidate available. It is typical that from beginning to end the job search should take at least two to six months for a candidate. Companies may look for two or three months before they go to offer, and if a candidate rejects their job, they will repeat the entire process again.

While this chapter about how organizations go about hiring people may seem disappointing, find solace in knowing that if your resume closely matches the open job, your odds of getting called go up dramatically. Some managers are extremely literal and if your skills aren't on the resume, they won't interview you.

Over the years I have gone to managers and asked them to consider a candidate although the exact skill was not presented on the resume, explaining that it was qualified and covered in the interview that I conducted. Often I was met with a skeptical eye as they reluctantly interviewed my candidate.

To prove my theory, I'd like to tell you about a client that worked with me in my coaching practice. He was looking for a General Manager position in another city and was not getting a lot of responses to his resume. After sixty days I knew something was wrong or he would've had calls by then. I decided to gather some data and see what qualifications an employer thought a General Manager needed. I went on www.indeed.com and found five jobs with that title. I cut and pasted qualifications and duties into a Word document, and then sat back to read them all. All five had several skills that were a must have in order to qualify for the job, telling me that those must be at the top of the resume and clearly stated. Those included P&L responsibilities, managing a team of people, monitoring customer satisfaction and visiting customers. Some stated they wanted some business development or closing skills. There was a clear theme in the postings, and I re-wrote the resume accordingly. Before long, the phone was ringing and he was getting interviews. He ended up with a good job as a Branch Manager of a service company in Houston, Texas.

Employers look at paper first, then people. This concept has always been odd to me because when I came into the business years ago, I was taught to hire people and not paper. Like it or not, from an employer's perspective, it is the other way around. Your resume gives you the red carpet and the opportunity to interview. The beauty of networking your way into a job is that the resume is irrelevant.

Above all, employers look for employees that will not become sources of HR issues in the workplace, which is why it is important to not only display competency in the interview, but also to be liked. People hire people who not only solve their problems, but also would make good company for lunch on a Friday afternoon. Although business and making money is the goal, business is only as good as the people doing it and how well they work together. This is why you will get rejected if the team does not like you. What you hear on the other end of the phone is that you are not a 'good fit', but this may simply translate to they did not like you, or worried they wouldn't work well with you.

While the hiring process itself is not a personality contest, being personable is an important component of getting hired. While this book advocates that you be authentic, just understand that being easy to work with is a factor in the hiring decision. The reason I encourage readers to be authentic is because if you choose the next job, and are happy, that energy goes into the position. Energy begets energy, be it positive or negative. When you give your best each day, that energy multiplies—for everyone. I have witnessed stock prices actually jump when the right team was in place in an organization. It's like an orchestra where the pieces all play together at the right time and tempo. There is nothing more powerful than that.

Jobs open because they have a problem to solve. If you can solve their problem and be personable while you do it, you will be chosen over a candidate who lacks the second part. Leaders above all want to know they can trust you. They want to know that you can do your job and never make them look bad. They need to trust you not to overstep, but to rise to the call of action.

All leaders want respect and control over their staff. During the interview, they are assessing this quality, or lack thereof, within you.

Research has shown that employers across the board in all industries look for the attributes listed below. My comments in italics expand on the hiring manager's thought process and what they're looking for in an employee.

Punctuality
It seems silly to comment on this, but managers have told me that this matters; it points to how much you care about the job and value the company. Being late shows them that you do not take your job or your career seriously. Punctuality also lets them know they can count on you. While lateness more commonly occurs with junior or entry level positions, it is something that is silently looked at with salaried employees as well.

Communication Skills
Communication skills can mean anything from how well you write emails to how you speak up in meetings, to talking through problems before they arise. The key is to understand how an organization uses communication and to determine what is acceptable. Some like email, others like meetings, and others use reports and data to communicate. However, across the board this is one of the most talked about and important attributes an employee must display. Quantity of information and when you give information is also important.

Work Ethic and Motivation

No employer wants a lazy employee. Work ethic does run on a scale between your Steady-Eddie employees and your type A drivers. Managers want to know that they can count on you to work late on a deadline and complete the project. Motivation will also figure into your ability to be promoted. At some point a manager will be concerned that if they do not promote you, the organization will lose you entirely to the competition.

Follow Through

Shortly stated, this is your ability to complete a task, preferably without being asked twice.

Dependability

While this may seem like a repeat of the above, dependability is the ability to predict what you will do over a course of time, from your performance, your quality of work and how many bad moods you have in a month. Managers like to know who to give the tough projects to in order to ensure they will get done.

Quality Work

Consistent quality work is something that every manager looks for in an employee. Having this quality lessons the chance of you working for a micromanager.

Professionalism

All managers appreciate a professional employee. Professionalism is the ability to act coolly under pressure, have appropriate responses when the line of questioning is difficult and not getting caught up in office gossip. These are considered, from a manager's perspective, 'low stress' employees. They never have to worry about being embarrassed by how you may respond.

Accountability

Managers have told me over the years, it's not what an employee did wrong; it's their ability to admit it, solve the problem and move on. Accountability allows you to say quickly and surely, "I made a mistake". Rarely does an employee get fired if they display this at-

tribute. Making mistakes is okay. It's what you do to correct them that counts.

Integrity
Integrity is not a subjective trait. It ranges between not stealing office supplies or taking long bathroom breaks, to not lying on your expense sheet. Integrity is the quality of being honest and trustworthy. Demonstrating integrity is the ability to consider the business needs first, and not your own needs.

Competency
Managers cannot stand it when they find an employee they hired to be incompetent. They don't want to make excuses for you because it's embarrassing, and a negative reflection on them.

Collaborative
This trait marks your ability to work with others in a team and to deliver your end of the bargain. If a manager asks for your input on how you could do your job better or faster, it shows that collaboration is a sought after quality.

Team Orientated (With the ability to work independently.)
This is the biggie. This dictates that introverts are forced into being extroverts and vice versa. This is the perfect balance of knowing that you fit into a bigger whole, and that you're capable of doing your part on your own.

The above characteristics come from literally thousands of interviews with the department managers, CEO's, CFO's, Engineering Managers and Project Mangers in charge of hiring people. These leaders always have a difficult time describing what they want outside of skills, but do emphasize the importance of 'fit.' From the headhunter's perspective, 'fit' is difficult to figure out since it is immeasurable and subjective to the employer. Telling me you want someone who is punctual and a good team player can mean anything. Giving specific instances as to why an employer fired the last guy gives me a better idea of what drives him/her crazy as a manager, and what s/he will not put up with from subordinates. Each company has a unique quality—an energy or vibe if you will, that resonates with the bulk of the staff.

For instance, Nike people are broke from a certain mold, and those employees may not necessarily fit another culture easily, regardless of their skill set. Nike people typically workout avidly or play sports. They are competitive and driven, but friendly. Bluntly stated: smokers don't apply there. Nike has a very distinct flavor and energy to it. Likewise, Intel or Microsoft has a different feel to it than Nike employees. My point is, you cannot always take a Nike employee and plunk them into another retail company because it may not work. The larger the organization is, the more diluted the skill sets of the individuals working there become.

While on the surface you might think that large companies contain similar skills, oddly enough the *type* of person that is drawn to each organization is vastly different. After the company culture fit is satisfied, the next challenge is finding the right energy to sync up to the leader's style and expectations. Each manager I have met over the years has different attributes they like to work with, and attributes they strongly dislike. Surprisingly, most leaders did not know they had such preferences until I met them.

Department managers secretly worry that you will make them look bad. Performing poorly or not meeting a deadline reflects on their ability to lead, in addition to the financial impact it has on the business goal. Retainment issues also reflect on their leadership, and they know it. High turnover is the kiss of death for the department manager. There can only be so many 'bad' hires before corporate starts to look at the leadership.

While I realize that this chapter covers a lot of information, from your perspective there are only two things you need to remember:

1) There is no job process in most companies where you apply and
2) Managers look for specific qualities from you, so be authentic to yourself, but aware of what an employer really looks for in a valued employee.

Recently I met with an organization that retained me as a consultant to advise them on their hiring process. To my surprise, during one of the meetings the owner stated, "You know it's difficult to hit on a good hire. Sometimes I get one from an ad or a referral, but it's difficult to really know if they will be good or not. In fact, thinking about all of our discussions and what you are suggesting, I realize that we have never had an actual hiring process before working with you. We never had a profile of the candidate or an exact target list that is focused to who we are looking to hire. And what's funny about that is I am an engineer that owns this company! I know about process, but never thought about that in terms of hiring."

Those are strong statements, and his organization is not unique. Many companies don't have a hiring process spelled out from the job description to interview questions to reference checks. This lack of process leaves your job hunt up to chance, at best.

From your perspective, when approaching an organization, assume that there is no hiring process.

Chapter 15

Snoopy Employers

While we talked about social media and how to use it, I'd like you to consider social media as a tool from the employer's perspective.

What are they thinking?

Well, know that the second your cover letter and resume hit someone's desk they will get online and Google your name. Although this was discussed in an earlier chapter, remember that employers will likely look at your LinkedIn account, read it, see who you are connected to and make all sorts of judgments about you. Here are some sobering facts:

In May of 2010, *The New York Times* reported that according to a study conducted for CareerBuilder.com by Harris Interactive, forty-five percent of employees questioned are using social networks to screen job candidates—that's more than double from a year earlier, when a similar survey found that just twenty-two percent of supervisors were researching potential hires on social networking sites like Facebook, MySpace, Twitter and LinkedIn. The study, which questioned 2,667 managers and human resource workers, found that thirty -five percent of employers decided not to offer a job to a candidate based on the content uncovered on a social networking site. More than half of the employers who participated in the survey said that provocative photos were the biggest factor contributing to a decision not to hire a potential employee, while forty-four percent of employers pinpointed references to drinking and drug use as red flags.

This does not mean the pendulum should swing in favor of eliminating your online presence altogether. In fact, there is something a little odd about not having a profile on LinkedIn, so if you don't, I suggest you get one. Facebook pages should be locked down, not allowing others to see your page unless invited. Ditto with Twitter. Watch what you tweet.

Consider the higher up you go, the farther you have to fall if your profile is viewed when in job search, or for that matter while you are employed. Nothing is sacred and employers, according to the above study, will not give you the benefit of the doubt. Employers may deem it unsavory if they find pictures of you doing shots at a bar. And perhaps if you are over fifty, you don't need them knowing you have a Harley.

It isn't good or bad. It just is. Know an employer will see these things and judge you.

Enough said.

Chapter 16
Reference Questions They Ask

Chances are good that a prospective employer will check your references. According to a survey by the Society for Human Resource Management (SHRM), more than eight out of ten human resources professionals said that they regularly conduct reference checks for professional (eighty-nine percent), executive (eighty-five percent), administrative (eighty-four percent) and technical (eighty-one percent) positions. Regular reference checks were less likely, but still probable, for skilled-labor, part-time, temporary and seasonal positions. Information routinely provided for a reference includes dates of employment, eligibility for rehire, salary history, and employability.

It occurred to me to write this chapter after I met with Laurel. After applying for months to nonprofit jobs, looking for part-time or contract work, Laurel finally got the call for an interview. The position itself was perfect for her and her needs. At sixty, she was not ready to retire, but did not want or need to work full-time. She did not have the energy in her to start a private practice, and did not want to think about the years it may take to build up a good referral chain in order to generate enough money to make the practice worth her time. I suggested that she call nonprofit centers directly and offer up her services on a part-time basis. Surely, if they had the grant money, they would be interested in someone with her skills.

We met two days before the interview and I coached her on what to expect the employer to say. While Laurel took notes, I realized the most important thing I should mention is that she reach out to her references and warn them they would be getting a call. Predicting that Laurel was very close to a job offer, I wanted to make sure that the references returned the calls to HR in a quick, timely manner. Laurel left with her notebook full of scribbles from our conversation, and the intent to call her references that afternoon to give them a heads up. All of them agreed to help her out if the call came.

A few days later, HR did extend an offer for a part-time job, and Laurel was thrilled. Acceptance of the offer would be complete after the references were checked, and to Laurel's surprise she found that one of her references did not return HR's calls, putting her in a predicament. Laurel had to come up with another reference for HR and apologize for the delay. Embarrassed, she hoped that the mishap would not cause the employer to be suspicious of her performance, or worse, pull the job offer entirely.

While this chapter is written from the employer's perspective, I wanted you as the reader to understand what happens during a reference check. Information uncovered will make or break your candidacy, and while some employers will not disclose specific details out of fear of being sued, most will.

I have always been amazed at what kind of information I can pull out of a reference and how things like long pauses or the tone in their voice will tell me how well-liked an employer was. Like the previous chapter about managing your references, keep in mind these are the exact questions your reference will be asked—about you and your performance.

Here is a sample of reference questions that are asked by phone. This is a very typical list, but the questions may be more or less extensive, depending on the organization and the caller performing the reference check. Reference checks can be as quick as ten minutes or as long as half-an-hour.

- Describe how you worked with the candidate. Did s/he report to you?
- What was her/his position? Can you describe the job responsibilities?
- How would you describe his/her performance?
- How was the quality of work? Please elaborate.
- Absenteeism. Did s/he miss a lot of work? Was s/he frequently late?
- Were there any issues you are aware of that impacted her/his job performance?
- Did s/he get along well with management and co-workers?
- Was s/he promoted while with your company?
- If not, were they given additional responsibilities?
- What is the best way to lead him/her?
- Did s/he supervise other employees? How effectively?
- If I spoke to those employees, how do you think they would describe her/his management style?
- How did s/he handle conflict, pressure and stress?
- How did s/he take feedback?

- What is his/her strength? Limitation?
- What was his/her biggest accomplishment while working for your company?
- Would you rehire him/her if the opportunity arose?
- Do you think s/he would be good for this position?

For some organizations, this is a last step just to complete the file, after they have already made a hiring decision. It's more of a formality. For other organizations, the reference check is a place to 'prove' or uncover why you would be a good fit. Interviewers are looking for the good, the bad and the ugly in the reference. Personally, I know that no one is perfect, and knowing the ugly allows me to get a reality check regarding who I am about to hire, and have to deal with, after the first ninety days. Rarely have I had a reference check go bad, but this is the place for due diligence, just like the background checks and drug tests.

Most managers like references to be from someone you reported to in the past. While it is nice to have your direct reports comment on your leadership, or the coworkers that worked with you on the last project, their words don't hold enough weight to make a solid judgment. References are given and called upon for confirmation of what the employer saw during the interview, and not necessarily for a cheerleading session about how great you were to work with from the guy in the next cube over. Every employer out there raises an eyebrow if all the references given are from coworkers or indirect managers, such as project managers. They fear that you're hiding something.

For college grads, starting out on your first professional job without references from a previous employer, here is a piece of advice. Don't list your aunt, uncle, mother, father or siblings as references. Those don't count. Instead, ask your professor for a reference. Certainly, s/he can comment on your commitment to and passion for your studies. Don't be ashamed if you held a little part-time job at a sandwich shop while in school, as this displays some level of work experience. List those managers as references. They can comment on your attendance, work ethic and willingness to learn new skills.

Our first job teaches us a lot, and I think we forget that. They are the training wheels of life that allow us to demonstrate follow-through, commitment and just plain ol' showing up for life. These attributes, as small as you might think them to be, are important to the next employer, where you'll have the 'real' job. Each day that you show up to work, work with others, and get a weekly paycheck adds to your career experience. Never underestimate the power of a part-time job while in college. The work habits you develop there will be with you throughout your entire career, for they are the building blocks.

Along with reference checks, background checks are another important part of any employer's process. Employers can, with your signed approval, run a background check on you prior to hiring you. Generally, background checks are searching for 'hits' on your background, and, specifically, felonies. The background checks that I am most familiar with in the United States will search through twenty-one states. I'm not sure why the service doesn't check all fifty, but it is certainly enough to uncover any unsavory facts about a candidate in question.

Most background check forms will ask you for your approval and will also give you a line to disclose if, when they run the check, they will find anything suspect. This is not the time to lie, but know that if you answer 'yes' and explain, chances are the HR Manager will not run the check and will instead put you in the Do Not Hire file. Regardless, nothing aggravates an employer more than spending the fifty bucks on the background check only to find you have a DUI back in Nineteen Ninety-five. In some cases it's not the DUI that prevents you from getting hired; it's the fact that you didn't disclose and made them run the check. An old boss of mine used to say, "What part of being thrown in the back of a police car with handcuffs did you forget when you signed the form and checked the box no you didn't have any felonies?" Uh, good question.

I've seen people's choices come back to bite them. Years ago I had a young candidate come to me on referral. He was an accountant that was laid off from his CPA firm and found himself in the middle of a recession without a job. Thinking I could place him immediately, I agreed to interview him. Like all candidates, he signed the background check form after our meeting and I ran the check. No one was more surprised than me to find that his background check pulled a grand theft auto in Florida. Picking up the phone, I wondered what part of stealing a car and ending up in the back of a police car he forgot to disclose to me during our meeting.

Secondly, I started to wonder about his CPA license, knowing he would be unable to get one after the charge was confirmed. When pressed, Neil stated that he didn't think the background check would pull the felony and he didn't steal a car.

That was when the whole story came out. When he was in college, he went out drinking with a buddy for most of the night. At four AM, they stumbled across campus and got the bright idea to take a golf cart for a joy ride. Normally, campus golf carts were locked down and only used by security, but on this particular night they were unlocked. It was not long before the campus police pulled them over. It just so happens that in the state of Florida if you steal an automobile valued over 2,000 dollars, it is charged as grand theft auto. His friend went on to get hired at PriceWaterHouseCoopers, but did not pursue his CPA.

Clearly, they neglected to run a background check on him or they never would have hired him. I shared with Neil that at some point, even his friend's number would come up and his partners would find out about the event. Inevitably, the partners of the firm would put pressure on him to obtain his CPA, for which he would not qualify due to the felony. Neil had to face the fact that the prank he did years ago may cost him his career and would stall his next job. Most employers, particularly in economic recovery, will pass on the grand theft auto accounting candidate in search of someone more reputable.

I gave Neil the same advice I would give any young person in this sort of predicament. Keep applying and tell the potential employer the truth. Be accountable when you tell the story, and let them know that you have paid the price and learned from the experience. Someone will understand and take a chance on you. Also know that what you did in the past will follow you on the background check forever, and with each job change, you will be forced to tell that same story.

Credit checks, on the other hand, are a whole other story. Most companies do not run these, while others do. They are mostly looking for slow payments on your charge accounts and bankruptcies. This becomes a real issue right after recessions for employers if they adhere to a strict policy on the credit check because it is not uncommon for a good employee to make late payments during tight times. This little fact then becomes a blemish on their record only to be uncovered two years later when the economy turns around and they are looking for another job. It's a shame when they get kicked out of the running. Many times I've stood up for these candidates. It never made sense to me to run the credit check in the first place. I can see the importance if you are a CFO or seeking a career in the accounting department, but in most positions within a company this information is irrelevant to how they will perform on the job. However, each company can make their own choice about who they want to employ, and what their hiring practice is in the HR office. No employer can run this check without your signed approval. And, you are expected to disclose anything that may surface on the report prior to them running the check.

While reference checks and background checks are common, so is pre-employment drug testing. Over eighty percent of Fortune 500 companies require drug and alcohol testing. These companies understand that substance-abuse costs industry over 165 billion dollars annually in loss of productivity, theft, accidents, absenteeism, increased workers' compensation, and health-care. Again, these tests cannot be run on an individual without their consent, and the form asks that the candidate disclose any prescriptions or drug use.

Each organization does its pre-employment screens differently. Some conduct the tests prior to offer, while others go to a formal offer letter with the contingency of passing the tests. Regardless, honesty is the best policy when filling out the forms.

Part Three
US (The Headhunter)

Chapter 17
Wish a Headhunter Would Call?

You will never be the same after you read this chapter.

This chapter looks at the hiring process through the lens of a headhunter; the individual who is supposedly paid to market, vouch for, and place you with the right company. Jobseekers often turn their power over to the headhunter, thinking that they can magically find them the job and open the doors of opportunity better than we can for ourselves. Job seekers align themselves with headhunters hoping to leverage their contacts and dodge applying online. It's considered a service-orientated business, with the headhunter acting as a matchmaker between companies and candidates, but the experience is often far less than that of a service. Regardless, these next chapters will help you to understand their motivations and how you can best manage the relationship.

This chapter should clear up a lot of misconceptions about the recruiting profession and what happens to you, the jobseeker, in the business relationship.

Mari was confused when she applied to jobs online through a recruiter and never heard back. While she submitted her resume to jobs for which she was qualified, her phone never rang.

From a headhunter's perspective, Mari may not have been what they were looking for in talent, and s/he didn't bother to tell her. While this may seem rude, recruiters cut people loose without telling them why. Headhunters are very focused on filling jobs, and often will not give the common professional courtesy to tell you if your resume is flawed, even when you may possess the necessary skills. If you find that you're taking time out of your day to meet with a recruiter and not getting calls for open jobs, consider following up after you send the resume, and directly asking what they think about your resume and skill set. Resumes, from a headhunter's perspective, should be concise, and address the must-have skill set they posted in the ad for their client. They will take time out of their day to pore over resumes. Shockingly, what takes you two hours to write on your resume will be read in about ninety seconds and will quickly end up in a yes or no pile on their desk. Without getting feedback from the headhunter to see if you are attractive on paper, it's hard to judge what's happening. Either they are lazy and dislike your resume, or it needs a re-write to better highlight your skills and make you more marketable.

Furthermore, headhunters will not call if there are glaring errors on the resume. Many years ago, a candidate of mine nearly cost herself a job because of a typo. It's hard to believe, but using an "e" instead of an "i" nearly cost her the interview. Embarrassed, I explained to the manager that she was, in fact, worthy of a conversation. These small errors will discourage a headhunter from calling altogether. My mistake was that I didn't find and fix the typo before sending it off to the client.

There is an expression in the business that while unkind, really paints the picture of what a headhunter-candidate relationship is all about. Headhunters will deem applicants "fee paid" candidates or "non fee paid" candidates. Yes, you are a fee to them, but we will get more into those relationship dynamics in the next chapter.

Fee paid candidates are people possessing top marketable skills who are highly desirable, or who present their skills (interview) very strongly. Meaning: they can close the job themselves if you can just get them in front of the manager. When they have the skills and are personable, a headhunter can get the deal done and make the placement!

For example, when I had candidates with direct internal audit experience, I knew that my clients would want to know about them. If a candidate came out of a particular school, with an MBA in finance and fifteen years of experience, I knew I could make ten calls and place them—and I did! Some skill sets are harder to come by than others, and I knew which people I could place immediately. This meant money in the bank, and I blocked out an hour in my morning specifically to call *those* candidates. This also gave me a sense of the market and how many jobs would be open and available for them. They were fee paid candidates. However, these candidates did not know this about themselves. Instead they thought me industrious. The truth of the matter was I just wasn't stupid, or lazy.

Sadly, on the headhunter's desk there is also a short pile of non-fee-paid candidates. While these were probably good citizens, they were people I couldn't place for a myriad of reasons. One gentleman had a DUI and couldn't pass the background checks. Another woman had a sketchy job history and had never held a job longer than two years, which the headhunter doesn't want to explain. You get the point….while they may have been *good* candidates, they were not *top* candidates.

A long time ago I was taught that top candidates are always working, even in recession. It took me ten years and two recessions to test that theory, but I found it to be true. Sometimes, if you looked deep enough, there was a reason why you could not get a fee for a candidate. Rather than waste their time or insult you, a headhunter just doesn't call back. They prefer to move on and find the next kill.

Remember the reality of your working relationship with the headhunter. *You are a fee to them.* If you go on an interview and reject the job after it went to offer, they will not likely work with you again. Their trust is gone and they will not want to put another opportunity in front of you for fear that you will do the same thing again. They will not allow you to shop jobs, so if you aren't interested in the position, tell them and don't go on the interview.

As strange as this sounds, some headhunter's don't know what you do, so they won't bother to call you for the job. You would think that a headhunter is paid to understand your skill set and know how to place you, but I have often found the contrary. Technical candidates with resumes that are too detailed or complicated—or worse, full of company acronyms—do not get called. If a headhunter cannot understand it, they move on. And, if you have the misfortune of getting caught on the desk of a junior recruiter who is not experienced enough to read your resume, they will not call at all. Remember, the headhunter's function is to bill, and bill quickly. If they cannot understand the resume, they'll move on to a candidate they can place in the interest of time and money. Dead air from a headhunter can only mean two things: either they don't work with your skill set, or they don't know how to read your resume.

Walt, a client of mine, was an Electrical Engineer with an excellent skill set. To his disappointment he figured out that the recruiters at a local Los Angeles agency did not understand what he did, even after he took time out of his day to interview with them. I told him that he only had a couple of choices.

He could educate them on titles and jobs to look for on his behalf, or drill down and ask them to be honest. If they don't ever fill his skill set, he needed to know and to find another firm.

Take some time to understand the agency and headhunter that you will be working with, and treat it no differently than you would if you hired a realtor. If you were selling a house, wouldn't you want to list it with a top producer? Of course! You would want someone experienced in the area you wanted to buy the next house in, and you would want to know that they could handle your listing and get your place sold within a few months. You would also feel a level of comfort in listing with someone who has a keen knowledge of the housing market overall, including what types of places sold quickly, which ones didn't, and why. You would enjoy working with them because they could provide the service of selling the house, and educate you in the process. Furthermore, you would be curious to know how many years they had been selling houses.

Why would working with headhunters be different? Who you work with should be even more important because your resume is a statement of your career, skill level and reputation in the business community. Find out the background and credentials of the headhunter you work with, their level of interest in your skill, and if and when they think they can place you. That is a fair question to ask; after all, you want some level of comfort about tim- ing since you would be making the job change. That question also flushes out whether they work with people like your or not. The job seeker is a slave to the market *and* the open positions on the headhunter's desk.

Like it or not, you are a product. You are bought and sold. One agency I worked for years ago liked to call themselves "skills brokers". I guess that is a fair title. We knew the market, what it would bear in salaries, and what skills were in hot demand. We were honest with candidates and I was one of the few out there taught to directly tell a candidate that I was not their best resource and/or that I had no intention of placing them. This hard news delivered gave the candidate fair expectations. When I was in the business, I was honest. If the resume needed improving, I told them and gave them a few minutes of coaching. I made myself available, and told them what I thought.

Even when I did not place them, I left the working relationship nicely. No one left my office wondering where s/he stood.

Most headhunters do not operate like that, and this is why the headhunting profession itself can get a bad rap. You cannot blame the headhunter for your career choices or even their lack of ability to find you a job. There are good headhunters and bad ones. At the end of the day, it's the candidate's responsibility to choose who they work with and shop jobs. Remember, no one can make you happy but you. It's up to you to manage your career and your choices.

I warn all candidates. Buyer beware. Know who you are working with when you send your resume over in an email. You must entrust your career to someone who earned that trust, and that will work for you to find you the right job.

After all, this isn't about finding just another job, is it?

It's about finding the <u>right</u> job!

Chapter 18
Headhunters Aren't (Necessarily) Your Friends

This is the gritty truth about the headhunting profession, and is not for the faint of heart.

First of all I strongly encourage you to stop thinking that a headhunter is your friend and wants to find you a job. They are not your friends. Blind faith in someone else, particularly someone that is actually a stranger and motivated by money, can easily lead to disappointment. Never turn your power over to someone completely. Giving up your power is like signing a form from your attorney that you didn't read completely, assuming s/he would protect you. What's worse is that trusting the wrong headhunter with your career could be downright dangerous. The last thing you need in a job search is to have your current employer find out that you are looking, and if a recruiter email blasts out your resume all over town, that scenario is likely.

This is not to say that working with a headhunter is bad. They are not all bad and frankly it's wise to go with one or two that you have researched and that you trust. My original suggestion in this book was to look at the job search as a tiered process where you would look at opportunities yourself, add a recruiter to the mix and construct a target list. Understand what a recruiter is supposed to do. They are not your counselor; they do not have a magic wand and are not responsible for getting you the job.

At the end of the day, they are responsible for finding the opportunity, and if you are lucky and you have a good headhunter, they will coach you through the interview process. But that is about it. Their job ends with finding you the opportunity to interview. Your job begins by nailing the interview and getting the offer. Know the line where their job drops off, and yours begins.

Understand how headhunters are compensated, because that alone will burst any fuzzy bubble you have in your mind about them liking you or being on your side. They don't. They want to bill you. They need to bill to keep their job. This is not a personal relationship, it's a business relationship, and it is best to know the difference. If you get confused trying to figure out if a relationship has an emotional attachment or not, just look and see if there is money involved. Since your salary and their compensation are involved, it's safe to bet that this is a business relationship. You are not going to invite them to your child's baptism after you land the job. Be clear in your relationship with them and do not allow them to manipulate you emotionally.

Understand clearly that when you walk into their office they are calculating you as a fee that goes into their pocket. Their job is to bill for the firm, so they have to know whether or not they can 'sell' you and your skill to a client. They look at your resume for marketable skills, and then proceed with their interview process. If you are not personable, or as we used to say, 's/he doesn't present well to a client', the headhunter will do little with your file and is not likely to not call you back. Notice I said file. For many headhunters you are not a person at all. You are merely an application on their desk with a reference sheet attached. There are a few exceptions in the profession, but generally speaking this is business as usual.

A good headhunter is willing to pick up the phone for you and call their book of clients to see if they can place you, whether they have an open job with the company or not.

This is a surefire sign that the headhunter is motivated to work with you, and deems your skill set (and your presentation) marketable. They also trust you in front of their clients and expect not to be embarrassed. Do right by them. Even if you don't get the job, they will likely find you another opportunity. After all, they have financial motivation that makes them want to place you.

The low producing headhunter exists, and you can recognize him/her by the fact that you're not seeing a lot of action. If you ask questions about the market and you get vague responses, that's another sign that they're green in the profession. Statistically, only one out of a hundred recruiters lasts beyond the first six months. Most wash out because this is a sales job, not a feel good job. Those recruiters quickly shift into an HR role and spend the rest of their career in corporate America. Really good headhunters will be in the field at least two years, and the best are in the field for ten years or more. Ten years is the breaking point, this is when many driven headhunters go out on their own and hang a shingle. The more senior in tenure, the more they have seen in the job market. Do not discount the old dogs for the young ones; thinking the young recruiter is 'hungry'. Being hungry doesn't get the job done. Being honest, tenacious and productive does. Remember, the old dogs also have years of relationships established and know through experiences which companies are good to work for and which are not. Leverage the contacts in their database.

Furthermore, recruiting is no easy job, and I think most people assume it to be a snap. You get a job order; you match to candidates and bill, right? That would work if your product was a box of nails and not people. Add the people dynamic and you get all sorts of things that go sideways. While headhunting may be a high paying profession, it is well paid for a reason. It's a lot of work. Even on the easiest day (and I've had few), the job itself is like changing your oil or mowing your lawn. Yeah, you can do it, but don't want to. Hiring for companies is the same way. Hiring is a pain. It is time consuming and frustrating. Companies will pay a headhunter's fee to get out of the hassle. They pay for a headhunter's contacts, services and their guarantee in the contract.

There is a signed contract, between the headhunter and the employer, referring to your placement. As a candidate, you should know how a headhunter is compensated. All headhunters are paid either by the client, or the company. The company comes to them and agrees to pay a percentage of your annual salary with a guarantee. Industry standard is twenty to twenty-five percent of the annual salary with a three-month guarantee. The guarantee states that if you are incompetent, quit suddenly or no show for work, the fee is guaranteed and the headhunter will replace. Some firms replace on a percentile basis, taking their money and prorating it by the days you worked and then giving a discount back. Others will not give a partial refund and keep the entire fee, but promise to replace immediately. Guarantees can go anywhere from six months to a solid year, and can be negotiated by the client. Typically, a client will ask for a longer guarantee if they fear that the skill set is impossible to replace in the current market, and will take time if the person quits or does not work out.

With tens of thousands of dollars worth of fees on the table, the headhunter has a lot of motivation to fill orders. They are client focused, and not candidate focused, no matter how nicely they treat you. Keep that in mind.

This is why I suggest a candidate be upfront and direct. Ask the headhunter if they think you will be placed, because as the candidate you have a right to know either way.

Contract positions are billed differently. They are billed in small amounts of money over time that adds up. Pennies are collected on the dollar for an agency, so if you ever accidentally see your bill rate on an invoice, do not think the agency is greedy and you should get more. What you may not understand is that the hourly bill rate for you includes all your taxes. The client will pay this gladly as they do not have to supply health benefits. Some agencies pick up medical and others do not. It depends how large the firm is and who you contract for. A headhunter will have a lot of motivation to keep the contractor, because contractors are hard to find and hard to keep. Most good ones get offered the full-time job, meaning the recruiter loses the billing. In my last firm, I had contractors working for one company for two years before someone in accounting figured out they were still getting billed. Eventually, as the job market turns from recession to bull market, the accounting department examines contractors and the fees they're paid. If the contractor has been there a long time, it becomes more reasonable for the client to just offer them a full-time job.

I have met individuals that hated their contract job and were miserable. When this happens, it's up to the recruiter to manage the complaint and talk to the employer for you. Being a contractor is confusing because while you sit in an organization, at the end of the day, the paycheck has the logo of the agency on it. Don't get confused about where your loyalty should be. You work for the agency, not the employer. And the agency works for the employer, not you.

From your perspective, understand what a headhunter does for a living, which may make them act outside of their integrity. When fees from clients are scarce or talent is tight, they may say or do things to force a placement. Social media and networking has also given the headhunter untimely competition that they didn't count on. Thirty years ago, you called a headhunter for their contacts. Now with LinkedIn and other social sites, the hiring manager can search for talent himself. Some companies consider headhunters the high paid middlemen they'd rather cut out of the deal.

Understand that the headhunter could become more focused on billing and getting their commissions, rather than on committing to partnering to find you the right job. When that happens, it's because the headhunter fears for his/her own job. It's best to work with a headhunter that is consultative and approaches things in a problem-solving manner. If at any time you feel pushed into taking a job you don't want, fire the headhunter immediately and find another one. Drive your own career and never give over the steering wheel to someone else.

My parting line is that the headhunter/candidate relationship should be balanced at all times, and that responsibility ultimately lies with the candidate. At the end of the day, everyone should win. The employer gets a great employee like you to start in two weeks, you get a great job that's a different and more positive experience than your last job, and the headhunter gets paid a fee for a job well done. No one should come up shorthanded.

Chapter 19
Always a Bridesmaid, Never A Bride

Mike called me this morning to say he was frustrated. After moving through three interviews for a job he was very interested in, the news came from the employer that he wasn't selected. Although he had asked the headhunter if they were talking with other candidates, he was left with the impression that he was the most qualified for the job. From what I could tell after listening to his story secondhand, it certainly sounded like he would go to offer. The job process itself left him irritated, and wondering why he was second best in the running. I call this the "Always a Bridesmaid, Never a Bride" syndrome.

The good news is that if you're making it to the interview stage, we know (from data and experience) that your resume is correct and well received, or you wouldn't be getting calls at all. We also know that if you can get through the first pass of the interview chain you can likely be invited to the final interview. But for some candidates it falls apart somehow after the second round. The real issue becomes closing the deal. This leaves the candidate with the sense of being second best, and it feels as bad as getting picked last on the dodge-ball team in middle school. With a dented ego, they are left to wonder why, often with little, if any, feedback from the manager. Short answers like 'You weren't a good fit' don't instill confidence. I'm here to give you a headhunter's perspective on what takes place, and hopefully remove some roadblocks for you.

The process is simple. The headhunter asks for your resume, selects the right job and sends it over to the manager for review. Hiring managers then 'shop' for talent, and interview five to seven qualified candidates. Trust me on this one; it's as irritating for the headhunter as it is for the candidate. Headhunters want to bill and give someone the job. We know that having more people in the mix makes the decision harder and the process longer, for you and for us.

Perceptions that the employer picks up in the interview process stick with them, and could lead them to believe the other guy is just 'better'. Perceptions are subtle little clues left behind that mean nothing, but end up being like the weight of a mountain of doubt in their mind. Once they make up their minds that there is something 'wrong' with *you* and the other candidate is just 'better', there's little the headhunter can do to change their minds. Be authentic, but be aware enough to throw an antenna out there to sense how the employer feels about you.

While I'm not suggesting that people embellish on the truth, or be overly cautious in the interview, it is prudent to practice interviewing before you go live. Talking out loud can help you identify pitfalls in the interview conversation. One client of mine practices in the car on the way to work, speaking aloud and trying out different responses. Others ask friends to prep some sample interview questions and practice with them.

It's safe to say that overall, employers want to know three things aside from your skill set right up front in the interview.

First, they want to know why you are looking, secondly, they want to know why you left your last job, and lastly they want to know why you want to work for them. Employers want a sense of security. They need to know that you make your career decisions carefully, and that your overall path has been thought out. In reality, that may not be your story. Very few people I've met have actually thought about their next job in some strategic manner. However, your resume tells a story on paper about who you are and where you've been for the last ten years. Taking jobs at a whim, or without an apparent career path guiding your choices, makes an employer downright nervous. The headhunter's job is to explain your career path to the client prior to them interviewing you.

You need to know your story.

You should be able to walk me through your interview within ten minutes, and tell me both why you left each job and why you're interested in a new one. While an interviewer doesn't need a lot of detail, they need to feel secure in your decision making process, including your choice of them. Remember, all employers want to be wanted and want to know why you choose them.

While the headhunter can gather feedback for you, it's wise to be able to ask an employer yourself. Clearly, if the candidate is getting rejected over and over again, something is wrong. Usually I can figure out what is 'wrong' if I run the candidate through a mock interview. In most cases, it's a simple case of wording. For example, if an employer asks the question, "What are your limitations?" and your response is "None." We all know that isn't true because we all have things we'd like to improve. Again, this is a perception left behind, like a piece of litter.

It's the employer's perception that matters at all times, not yours.

Think about what you're putting out there during the interview and how it will be received.

When an employer asks, "Why are you interested in this job?" and an interviewer replies, "Well, it's my last job and I'd like to retire from here.", that doesn't bode well with the manager. The perception is that this person is not as motivated as a younger, or shall I say, mid-career person who is about to buy a house and have their second child. While not a truth, it is a perception that hangs in dead air. A better way to answer would be, "I'm interested in your technology.", or "At this stage in my career, it's important to me to be a contributing team member." Although that sounds like fluff, it's a lot better than the original statement. Don't consider this lying, but rather as a re-packaging of information in a way that the employer can appreciate.

The other reason some candidates are not selected is for their lack of interest in the job. Frankly, if a qualified candidate displays an enthusiastic attitude toward the job and veers away from the 'what's in it for me' mode, they will bubble to the top. Showing genuine excitement for the company and for the job makes a glowing impression on the managers, leaving them with the sense that you'll care enough about the job if they hire you.

Asking a manager what the hiring process is, especially at second or third interview, is wise.

After the headhunter opens the door to an interview, ask the employer how many people they are interviewing and when they will be making a decision. Always feed that information back to the headhunter as a bone.

At the very end of the conversation, tell the employer sincerely that you are interested in the job, and leave it at that. It is not the headhunter's job to close the deal entirely. This little confirmation from you to the employer is needed. This gesture is not begging, nor is it horn blowing about what you can give to them. You are simply sending them the message that you will accept the position if it were offered.

Remember; it is not the headhunter's role to determine if this is the right job for you. While you can take their recommendations, you must make the final decision. Their job is to guide you, particularly through the maze of interviews, if you're having a tough time going to offer.

In the interview process, companies will give you buying signs to let you know that they're interested. These could be as simple as scheduling with you to quickly meet with the next round of people, or as direct as asking when you can start. Keep your eyes and ears open for these signs, they will guide you through the hiring process and allow you to gauge where you stand with them. After they flower you with compliments and buying signs, just make sure you actually want to work for them. This process is a two-way street.

If you're still not getting picked for the job, ask the headhunter for coaching. Any feedback is good feedback, and although it may sting, it will allow you to learn from the experience. However, don't be surprised if they don't give you direct answers. In most cases, they're merely acting polite in the interests of not hurting your feelings.

Chapter 20
Change Everything And Everything Changes

I know what I experienced.

I know that when people come to me in job transition and go through my program, they are never the same again. I think it's because changing a career changes your life. It's a subtle way of saying that you don't deserve to be treated poorly any more. It is a definite no-thank-you. Consider it a professional parting.

When relationships end, people change. They are forced into change and this transformation can spill over into other parts of their life. Ending a job is no different than ending a relationship, really. It is the parting of two energies that came together. Where there were two, there is now a void.

Over my years in career coaching within my own private practice, I've seen different people react differently to job changes. Some were very positive, and found that the job change allowed them more space and freedom to spend at home with family, or to pursue a hobby. The job no longer took up all of their energy, leaving them with the feeling of freedom. I used to think this was a mindset, but observed that this is far more than controlling one's thoughts. Being stuck in a job that you hate can wear you down. It can suck the life out of you. Some didn't even realize how depleted they were until they got out. It is the absence of pain. Released, they began to feel again, and they are no longer beaten down.

It's a shame that we have gotten ourselves to that place in relation to work, but most Americans are unhappy. CBS did a poll on work satisfaction among Americans and discovered that only fifty-one percent found their jobs interesting, where as in 1987, seventy percent of American's said they were interested. Since 1980, three times as many workers contribute to their health care program. All this data leads to this overall feeling of discontentment within American workers.

Neil Diamond Walsh states all change is for good, and no change comes about for bad. It's an interesting theory about transition. Looking back, I think everyone can attest to this. Such as the day someone got fired, which s/he used to look back on with bitterness and indignation, turned out to be the best day of their life.

Leaving a job often causes a tidal wave leading to cleaning up one's entire life. I knew one man who ended his job and ended up getting a divorce, which he initiated. Suddenly, the people at work start to remind you of the people at home and the abuse becomes intolerable. Taking the new job will change you, and there are no two ways about that. It's the slightest act of saying that you deserve something better, and then receiving it that leaves an imprint on the mind. When the people in the play show up as your coworkers, you begin to re-evaluate again. You size up who you are and who you want to be. You close the gap.

The longer you are in a job, the harder it is to leave. This usually stems from insecurities, thinking that another employer will not want you. Sometimes it's as simple as fear of the unknown.

Ellie was a good example of this. Ellie worked for one company for twenty-five years. She went from college, to an internship, to a full-time job. She got married and had two boys. She divorced. She bought a new car and a house. Her life ticked on, but her job remained constant, even though it didn't fit her. Two years before she came to me, she toyed with finding something else. She would try on the notion and set it back down again. Safety and stability were things she valued.

To her surprise, and mine frankly, one day her supervisor made it clear that she was pushing her out. She threatened to have Ellie's job eliminated by the end of the year. Ellie began to see the writing on the wall. Our first session was more about her letting go of the job rather than the actual mechanics of finding a new one. Can you imagine working for one company for half your life and knowing nothing else? Ellie had not interviewed in twenty-five years. She had no idea how to go about looking for a job, although she knew that today jobs were posted on the Internet and not in the paper. I found her to be one of my bravest clients. Witnessing her emotional process and attachment to the job was encouraging.

She grasped the homework I gave her with gusto. Within two short months, she was offered a new position.

One day I received an email from her saying that her boyfriend kept looking at her like an amputee about to be rolled into surgery. At home monitoring email on my Blackberry, I chuckled when I read this, but also knew something much deeper was happening. It was now impossible for her mate look at her the same way. Doubts began to fill his mind about her stability and commitment to him. He needed to be needed, but Ellie had just demonstrated that she was the creator of her own life.

I cautioned her that since she stood up for herself, her life would change. No longer the person suffering in silence, Ellie bravely and diplomatically quit. People around her were not used to her quitting, let alone seeing her stand up for herself. I didn't need to be there to know that her boyfriend was questioning his role in her life.

People around you will have a reaction to your departure. From coworkers to family and spouses, people will have reactions. Most of this has nothing to do with you or the job change. It has to do with them and their response to themselves. People will question their own life decisions through your bravery. When a top producer leaves a company, it sends a message through the department. People start to quietly wonder if there's another place out there that's better for them too. They feel left behind. Spouses see growth as threatening if they aren't keeping up at the same pace. Some spouses enjoy the drama of your job and your tales of office woe. Without those stories coming home each night, they start to question their role. Ending a job is no longer being a victim, and when that happens others can't perceive you as a victim. That can be scary for them.

Changing the job is far more than changing buildings. Be prepared for it to change your entire life.

Chapter 21

Unity

After presenting to a crowd of two hundred participants at the Dallas Fort Worth convention center, I saw puzzled looks on their faces. I have a funny way of doing that to people, and I'm always amused at seeing the wheels turn in their heads, made visible by the expressions on their faces.

To recap all of this information I've presented to you here, and tie it up in a neat bow, all you need to know is this:

Get along with others.

Have compassion and understanding for your boss. They're in the hot seat and are accountable for your actions. They must answer for you.

Getting along with the boss is an important lesson to learn. Done well, it could save your job and even prevent you from being next on the layoff list. It could get you a promotion, or more money.

But that's not why you should get along.

Go into work, give what you can, and leave for the day. When you give it your best, know that your work leaves an indelible mark. It's what you have to offer.

Everything you do affects everything else.

Always.

In all ways.

In the end, you will never wish you spent more time in the office. I distinctly remember my father sitting in a wheel chair three days before he died. He had a grand career and taught me a lot about follow-through, and about honoring my word and never taking things personally. He was an excellent model, although our relationship was tumultuous. During the morphine drip he never did talk about his career. His biggest concern was what he left behind, and if it was good enough.

He wondered about his offerings, not his accomplishments.

He was wise enough to know that there were many moments in his life when he didn't care about his offerings. All he had to do was look at me and see a painful reminder, in the flesh next to him, holding his hand while he suffered.

The role of father and little girl disappeared in those moments while I gave him verbal permission to die.

All of your American life you're taught that acquisitions and consolations are the most important. In fact, you spend the majority of the day trying to get what you're after—recognition, money, fame, sex, food, housing, status.

And right around forty-seven years old you wake up at 3am, look at the ceiling and wonder if work is what it's all about.

From zero to twenty-five you're figuring it out. What is school? Why is it important? What's job and how is it different from a career? What is relationship? Marriage? Children?

You kiss a boy or girl…and it all starts…the endless cycle of getting, getting, getting. Our degrees hang on the way as achievements encased. Accomplishments are purchased like your first house. You stack them up and naively believe that means you have a good life.

Like lemmings we follow along.

We kid ourselves by saying that the job is what gives our kids a better life, but why do we really do what we do? Why do we say what we say at work?

Eventually you wake up because the empty hole in your life is so big you can never fill it up. You're never satisfied and feel driven to exhaustion.

There is this small light that comes on when you realize that you're never happy, and that perhaps happiness is not located *outside*.

That's when you understand that the problem is the job—and you call me.

You are seeking another acquisition (job) and consolation. I am here. I listen.

Just know that changing the job may not be your issue.

There is a remote possibility that YOU ARE THE PROBLEM.

It's how you view the job and the boss that causes the issue; so before you pitch your job searching for something that is a 'better fit' for you, think it over.

It is the job?

Can you look at it differently?

Everything is temporary. Jobs, marriages, people, pets, houses and things—even your body is temporary. It is okay to decide you are finished with a job and move on. I'm not saying that it isn't.

But, if you leave this job and go someplace else, are you carting the same stuff with you, things like intolerance for others, arrogance, ego, or separation.

It doesn't really matter if you stay in this job or find another.

What matters is what you have to give.

I've said this many times at the podium: You have talent. You have something that no one else has. There is something that you can do that no one else can do. This is your talent. It is an expression that rises up inside you and produces something. You take that energy each day into your job in exchange for money. It is that simple.

Work isn't necessarily about producing a result. Sometimes it is the lesson of being of service. It's about being lost in the throes of creativity.

Know that when your boss has a bad day and says something sharp, it has nothing to do with you. It has to do with them. What you control is your response.

Response, my dear friend, is much different than reaction.

Get along with others at work.

Give what you have to give.

Let the rest fall where it may.

Acknowledgements

Shortly after I finished the book and the last chapter clicked into place, I realized this book is more of an offering, because in the end all I have to give is myself. My great teacher told me, the body is an apartment and the lease is running out. I understand that soon I'll be leaving. The time is now, and I feel urgency.

Here are a few acknowledgments that I'd like to make to people that have changed me forever.

Some days I don't even recognize myself.

Deep gratitude goes to Steve Lions Yoder. From the artwork on the cover, to the website and all of the talent that you share with me. I couldn't have done this without you. I appreciate that you graciously share me with the world. It is an honor and privilege to be your wife.

Thank you to Teresa Lieberman. You are an excellent expression for me to witness. You knew when to tell me to keep going. You told me it would be worth it. It was.

For my parents, now deceased, thank you for giving me life. I am determined to do something good with the life you breathed into me. It shall not be wasted, I promise.

For my two brothers, also gone from earth plane. We shared tribe, time and space. Tommy I miss you most.

To the Divine Mother and all her mystery, joy and creative force. May Maya be brief.

Heartfelt gratitude to Steve Sabine…thank you for everything!

My life will never be the same for I have new eyes.

Made in the USA
Charleston, SC
05 December 2012